GREGG SHORTHAND

Manual for the
Functional Method

by

LOUIS A. LESLIE, C.S.R.

Arranged in accordance with the
Anniversary Edition of Gregg Shorthand

THE GREGG PUBLISHING COMPANY

Business Education Division, McGraw-Hill Book Company, Inc.

New York   Chicago   San Francisco   Dallas

Toronto   London

GREGG SHORTHAND MANUAL
FOR THE FUNCTIONAL METHOD

Shorthand Plates Written by
WINIFRED KENNA RICHMOND

Aug. 1949-JC-20

PUBLISHED BY THE GREGG PUBLISHING COMPANY
Business Education Division of the McGraw-Hill Book Company, Inc.
Litho'd in the United States of America

FOREWORD

One of the most fascinating things about "the lithe and noble art of brief writing" is the infinite variety of methods that can be adopted in teaching it. For this reason I have always maintained a receptive attitude toward new methods of handling the subject. After all, the *system* is my main interest, and any method that promised to contribute to the attainment of better results in teaching it was deserving of consideration. We have published a number of different methods of presenting the system, and we shall probably publish others. Most of the methods we have published are marked by a difference of emphasis on certain phases of shorthand instruction, but it is my belief that after trial and comparison of all these methods, and of others that may be developed later, there will emerge a better-balanced plan of instruction than any that has yet appeared.

In his book, *The Teaching of Gregg Shorthand by the Functional Method,* Mr. Leslie said:

> Without his [Dr. Gregg's] supervision and, more important, his inspiration, I should never have been able to make this contribution to the advancement of methods of teaching shorthand. This method is the culmination of that advance begun by Dr. Gregg in 1888 in his first shorthand textbook. The shorthand system presented in that first textbook represented so tremendous an advance over anything previously published that it has obscured the fact that the method of presentation used in that textbook represented an equally great advance over previous methods of teaching shorthand—a great step in the direction of simplicity of presentation and ease of learning.

This is a very modest and, at the same time, a very generous statement. The fact is that the Functional Method is almost wholly the work of Mr. Leslie. It is true, of course, that in the course of twenty years of close association with me Mr. Leslie has become thoroughly familiar with my views about methods of shorthand instruction, and has followed closely the development of the various editions of the system in which these methods have been put into effect. To that extent only can I claim any credit for the origin or development of this method of teaching the system.

All the editions of our Manual have been marked by a trend toward greater simplicity in the presentation of the rules until, in the Anniversary Edition, the rules were almost eliminated, many of them being put in the form of explanatory footnotes. As the Preface to the Anniversary Edition said:

> Each revision marked a step forward in simplifying and popularizing the study of shorthand. Each revision has placed increasing emphasis upon the desirability of teaching shorthand as a *skill subject* from the beginning and throughout the entire course. This method enables the teacher to direct the maximum of effort toward the training of the student in actual facility in writing and the minimum of effort to expositions of rules and principles.

In the Functional Method Mr. Leslie has pushed two basic principles in my shorthand philosophy, if I may so term it, to their utmost limit. One of these principles is that of minimizing rule teaching and placing the emphasis on reading and writing shorthand. The Functional Method does not merely minimize the teaching of rules—it abolishes the study of the rules. The other principle is that at the beginning a student should not be asked to write anything in shorthand until he has a clear mental picture of what he is to write. In the Functional Method this Reading Approach is carried far beyond anything I attempted or contemplated.

The mental reservation I have about the Functional Method is that it seems to me that all reading practice should be supplemented by movement and penmanship drills. The clear visualization of the forms before writing them is important in the beginning, but there comes a time when mere visualization of the forms will not convey to the student the easy, rapid manner in which the forms and combinations are written by experts. As I said in the first chapter of *The Use of the Blackboard in Teaching Shorthand:*

> Textbook illustrations go much farther in real teaching than any amount of printed description. But they cannot go so far as the teacher goes in his illustrations on the board. The teacher can demonstrate movement, which is just as important as form, because form is the result of movement. This the textbook illustration cannot give. . . . Any teacher who is thoroughly versed in his art knows that there are forms for words, combinations, and phrases that have to be *shown,* if they are to be assimilated. . . . Blackboard outlines are going to make an impression. Seen with the eyes, they are going to be photographed on the brain, and from the brain transmitted to the hand.

In *The Teaching of Shorthand* I said: "Shorthand is largely *manual,* and the technique of execution can be most quickly secured by the imitation of correctly written forms placed before the student as illustrations. When you place a shorthand form on the board, your students instinctively *imitate the manner of writing* and the actual form of the word or phrase." Undoubtedly experienced teachers will take care to include such drills and illustrations in their class work.

Mr. Leslie deserves great credit for the skill with which he has developed his plan of teaching the system, and for the energy and enthusiasm with which he has advocated it. He has repeatedly urged that, owing to the lack of suitable materials, the Functional Method was being put into operation under a severe handicap, and that much better results could be obtained with it if such materials were provided. It is obvious that, from its very nature, the Functional Method requires a great quantity of reading matter, as well as the keys which are an essential part of the course. As it was, Mr. Leslie did the best he could by using practically all the reading books and keys available, but that meant a formidable array of books at a formidable cost. What was needed was a complete and compact course, arranged and graded in accordance with the Anniversary Edition of our Manual. We have now provided this material in two volumes, with a teacher's manual.

As the author of the system presented in these books, I hope that their publication will mark another step forward in the teaching of the subject.

JOHN ROBERT GREGG.

February, 1936.

A TALK WITH THE BEGINNER

Success in the study of shorthand, as with any other subject, depends largely on the effort made by the student *outside* of class. The teacher serves as a guide to the student. During the class period the teacher checks the work the student has done, to be sure he is on the right path, and explains what is to be done in order to help the student get the most value out of the time employed on study at home. A few suggestions are given here for your home study in order that they may be always available to the student.

Assignments 1 to 21 require only reading for home work. Each of these assignments begins with lists of words or phrases, which the teacher will place on the blackboard for concerted reading by the class. When doing the home work on that assignment the student should reread the lists of words or phrases and should then read the letters and articles which follow.

At the end of the book the student will find a transcript of the shorthand. This is included so that the student may cover the most ground in the shortest time. As soon as you hesitate on an outline, refer immediately to the printed transcript. Reread the lists and the connected matter with the aid of the key until you can read them fairly easily *without* the aid of the key. The more you practice reading, and the more fluently you learn to read this material now, the more rapidly and accurately you will be able to write shorthand when the time comes to begin writing.

Beginning with Assignment 22 you will be writing shorthand. Your home work for the rest of the assignments will be (1) reread the lists of words and phrases at the beginning of the assignment, (2) read the connected matter in shorthand, (3) copy into shorthand the connected matter which you have just read.

Always read the shorthand through from beginning to end before you write it. Never copy an outline without knowing the meaning. Refer to the printed transcript of the shorthand as often as you like, but continue to reread the shorthand until you can read the entire assignment once without having to refer to the key.

After you are able to read the shorthand easily, copy it in your notebook. Always write as rapidly as you can while keeping the hand under complete control. Aim at accuracy rather than speed, but do not *draw* the characters. From the outset, shorthand should be *written*. But you must remember that whatever you write must be read; hence the necessity for good penmanship.

As skill in executing the movements is obtained, the speed may be increased until the forms can be written accurately at a high rate of speed. Try to acquire a smooth style of writing; execute each character with an easy, continuous motion of the pen and pass directly to the next without unnecessary movements.

Each assignment in this Manual has been very carefully planned to require forty minutes for satisfactory completion by the average student. If the student needs more time to complete an assignment, that is usually a sign that he is not using the printed transcript of the shorthand properly. If the student is willing to spend more than forty minutes in attaining a higher degree of fluency in reading the shorthand in the book, he will be rewarded at the end of the course by a higher speed and greater accuracy.

Success in any study depends largely upon the *interest* taken in that particular subject by the student. This being the case, we earnestly hope that you will realize at the very outset that shorthand can be made an intensely fascinating study. Cultivate a love for it. Think of it as the highest form of writing, which is itself the greatest invention of man. Be proud that you can record the language in graceful lines and curves. Aim constantly to acquire artistic skill in executing those lines and curves. You *can*, if you *will*, make the study of shorthand a perfect joy instead of a task. Skill in the use of shorthand is a possession that has been coveted by the wisest of men and women, for it is not only a practical instrument in commercial work, but a much-prized and valuable accomplishment and a means of mental culture.

THE ALPHABET OF GREGG SHORTHAND

CONSONANTS

Written forward.

K G R L N M T D TH

Written downward:

P B F V CH J S SH

H NG NK

VOWELS

ă	○	ĭ	○	ŏ	◡	ŭ	◠
ä	◯	ĕ	○	aw	◡	ŏŏ	◡
ā	◯	ē	◡	ō	◡	ōō	◡

DIPHTHONGS

	Composed of				Composed of		
ū	ē-ōō as in *unit*			oi	aw-ē as in *oil*		
ow	ä-ōō as in *owl*			ī	ä-ē as in *isle*		

BLENDED CONSONANTS

The consonants are so arranged that two strokes joining with an obtuse or blunt angle may assume the form of a large curve, thus:

ten, den   ent, end   def-v, tive

tem, dem   emt, emd   jent-d, pent-d

CHAPTER I

Assignment 1

1. We are learning shorthand to save time. One way to save time is to leave out the letters we don't pronounce. In the word *knee*, the *k* and the final *e* may be left out because we don't pronounce them. Therefore, by writing simply *ne,* we have immediately saved one-half the time required to write the word as it is usually spelled. The word *cattle* is really pronounced *katl,* with only four letters instead of six.

Another way of saving time in writing is to write only as much of the longhand letter as may be needed to recognize it. Therefore, many of the shorthand letters are taken from the longhand forms.

2. In shorthand there are twelve distinct vowel sounds, which are arranged in four groups. Three closely related sounds are placed in each group. In this chapter we have the first two groups, which for convenience are named the A group and the E group.

THE A GROUP

ă	ä	ā
as in	*as in*	*as in*
mat	calm	came
m ă t	k ä m	k ā m

THE E GROUP

ĭ	ĕ	ē
o	°.	° ´
as in	*as in*	*as in*
kit	get	need
⌐	⌐.	⌐´
k ĭ t	g ĕ t	n ē d

Note: The first sound in the E group of vowels is the short *i*, heard in *din*, and should not be confused with long *i*, heard in *dine*, which will be given later.

The vowels are grouped according to similarity in sound. The large circle expresses three sounds of *a*. The short sound is unmarked, the medium sound is marked with a dot, and the long sound with a short dash. This system of marking is used in all vowel groups uniformly.

The dot and dash are occasionally needed to indicate the exact sounds in unfamiliar or isolated words, but otherwise they are seldom used.

3. The shorthand characters for *r* and *l* are taken from the ordinary longhand forms, as shown below:

The character for *a* in shorthand is the same as the *a* in longhand, except that we do not need the connecting stroke.

H is expressed by a dot written above the vowel.

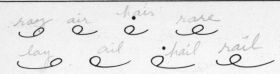

4. The shorthand characters for *n* and *m* may be remembered easily if you will simply underscore the longhand characters.

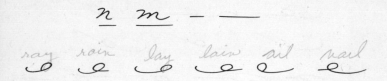

5. The shorthand characters for *k* and *g* come from the longhand letters.

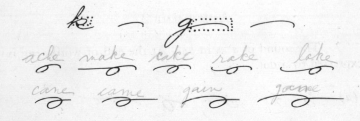

6. In shorthand, *t* is written ╱ and *d* is written ╱
As in longhand, *e* is a smaller circle than *a,* but in shorthand it is written without the connecting strokes.

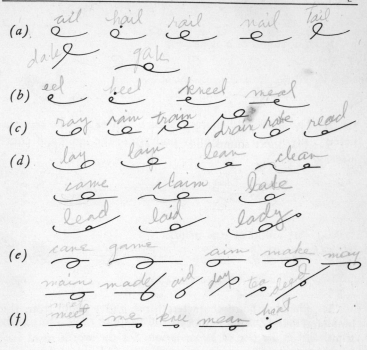

(a) *ail* *hail* *rail* *nail* *Tail* *dale* *gale*

(b) *eel* *heel* *kneel* *meal*

(c) *ray* *rain* *train* *drain* *rate* *read*

(d) *lay* *lain* *lean* *clean* *came* *claim* *late* *lead* *laid* *lady*

(e) *cane* *game* *aim* *make* *may* *main* *made* *aid* *jay* *tea* *feed*

(f) *meet* *me* *knee* *mean* *heat*

Assignment 2

7. The sound of *a* as in *hat*. At the end of words, *ing* is expressed by a dot.

(a) *hat* *adding* *have* *cat* *cattle* *nat* *nad* *nan*

(b) *hack* *tack* *rack* *lacking*

8. The sound of *a* as in *dark*.

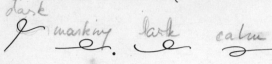

9. The short sound of *i* as in *hit*.

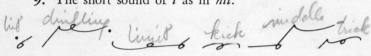

10. The sound of *e* as in *get*.

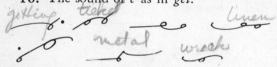

11. Brief Forms. Another aid to more rapid writing in shorthand is the use of abbreviations for the words most frequently written, just as in longhand we abbreviate *Mister* as *Mr.* These abbreviations are called "brief forms."

12. Phrase Drill. Many simple words may be joined, and you should become accustomed to making shorthand phrases from the beginning. In phrases, *they* may be expressed by *th* before *r* and *l.* With the brief forms you have just learned, you can write these phrases:

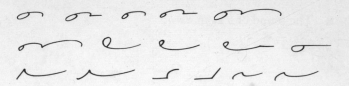

13. The sign for *t* is curved to express *th*, thus: ⌒ or ⌒

14. Punctuation. Period ﹨ paragraph 〉 parenthesis ( ) interrogation × dash ⫽ hyphen ⸝

15. Reading Exercise

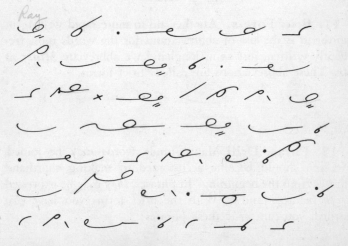

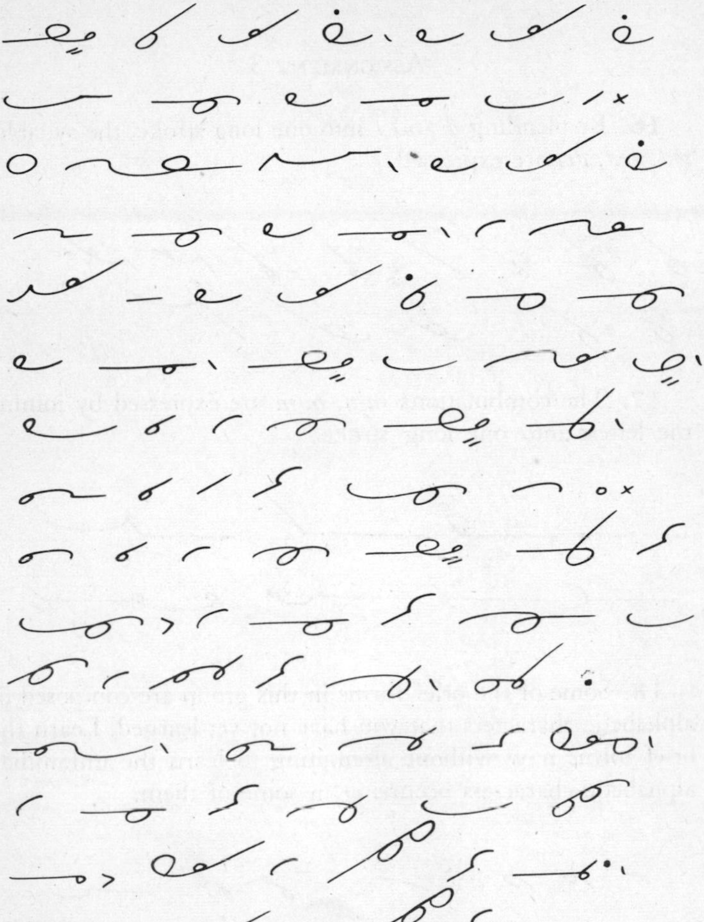

ASSIGNMENT 3

16. By blending *d* and *t* into one long stroke, the syllables *ted*, *ded*, *det* are expressed.

17. The combinations *m-n*, *m-m* are expressed by joining the letters into one long stroke.

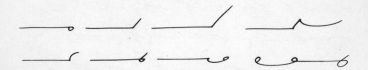

18. Some of the brief forms in this group are composed of alphabetic characters that you have not yet learned. Learn the brief forms now without attempting to learn the unfamiliar alphabetic characters occurring in some of them.

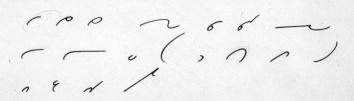

19. Reading Exercise

20. Drill on Previous Assignments

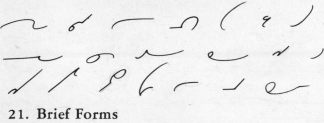

21. Brief Forms

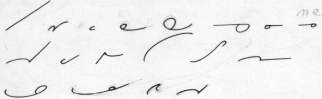

22. Phrase Drill. A circle is inserted in *did not* to make a ready distinction between that phrase and *would not*.

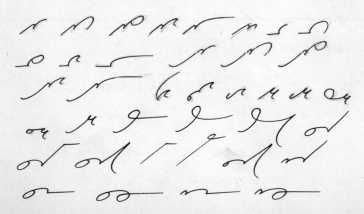

23. Reading Exercise

A COUNTRY INN

[Shorthand outlines]

CHAPTER II

Assignment 5

24. Drill on Previous Assignments

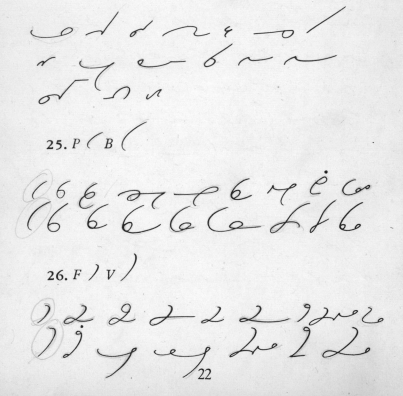

25. *P* (*B* (

26. *F*) *V*)

27. *Sh* / *Ch* / *J* /

[shorthand outlines]

28. Brief Forms

[shorthand outlines]

29. Reading Exercise

GETTING READY FOR THE FAIR

[shorthand outlines]

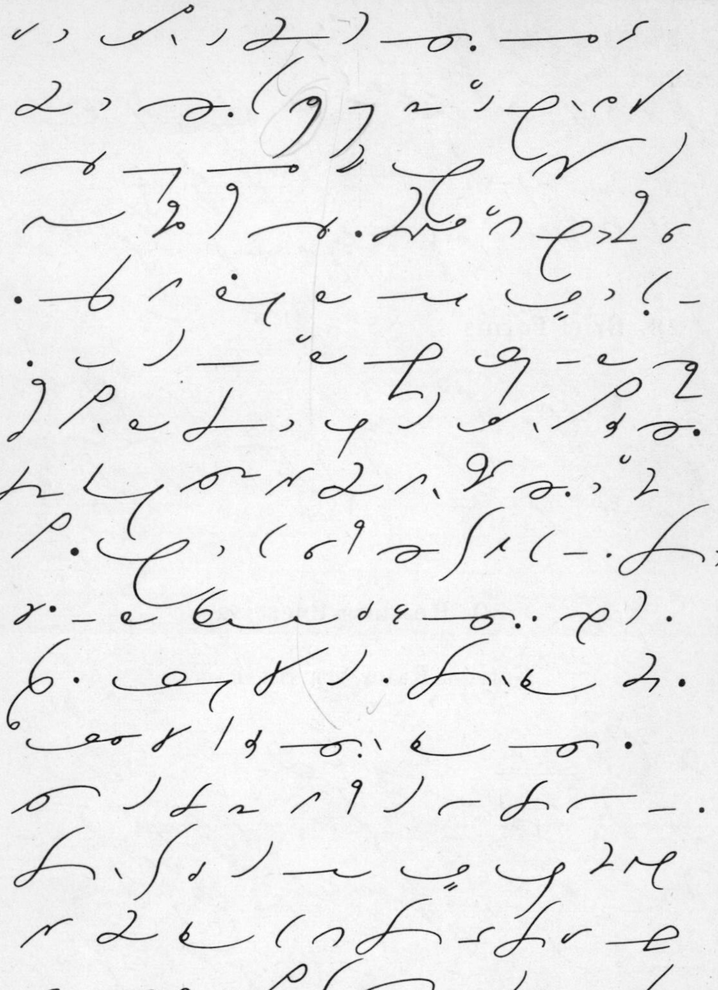

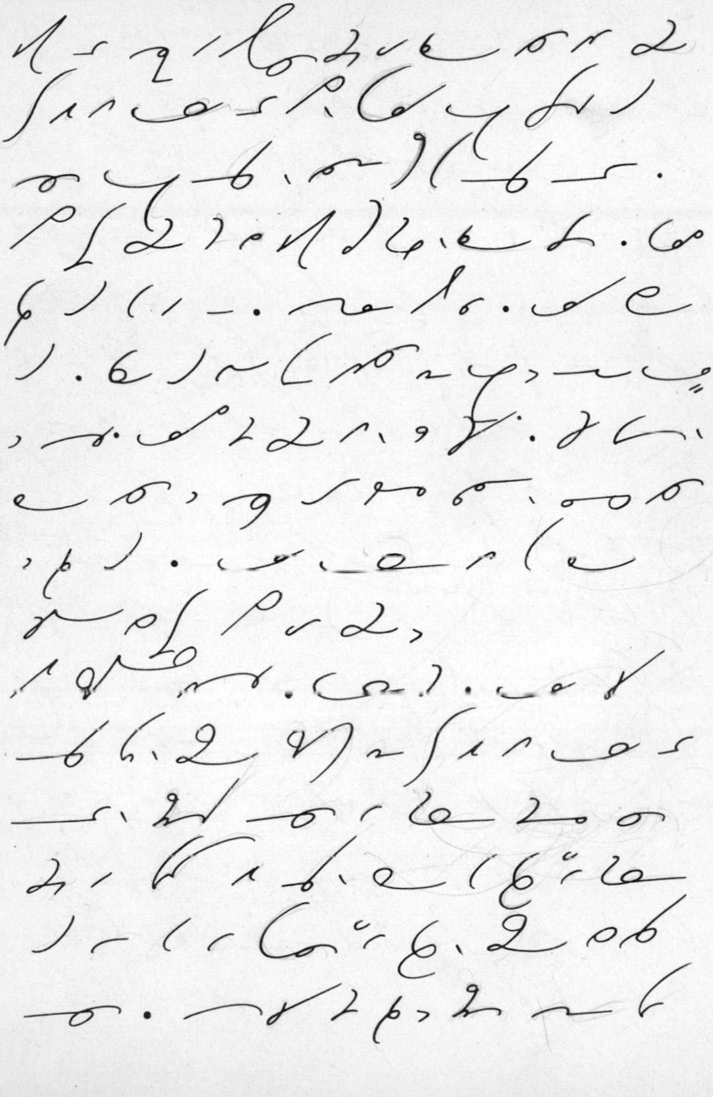

30. Drill on Previous Assignments

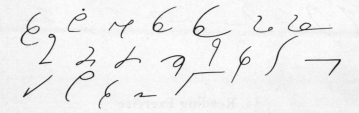

31. When *been* occurs in a phrase, it is expressed by *b*.

32. Phrase Drill

33. When *to* occurs before a downstroke, it may be expressed by *t*.

34. Reading Exercise

ASSIGNMENT 7

35. Drill on Previous Assignments

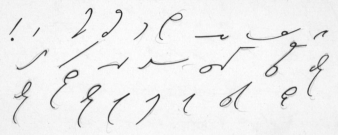

36. Two forms of *s* have been provided, so that an easy joining is always possible. The same sign is used for *s* and *z*. The following words illustrate the use of the left-motion *s*:

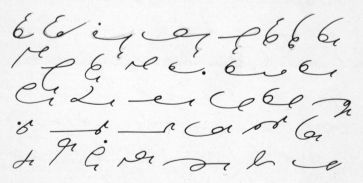

37. These words illustrate the use of the right-motion *s*:

[shorthand outlines]

38. Reading Exercise

SHIPPING GOODS

[shorthand outlines]

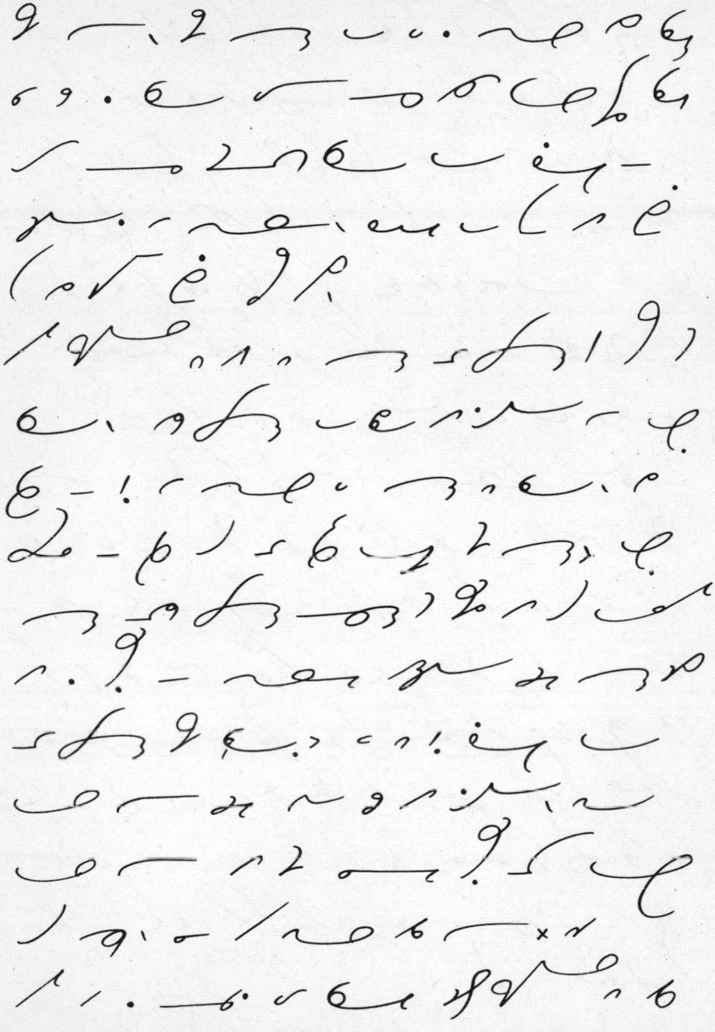

39. Drill on Previous Assignments

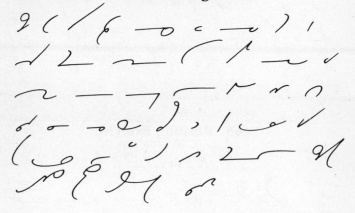

40. When the two *s* signs are joined, they blend together.

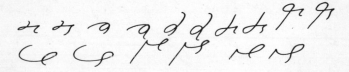

41. Brief Forms

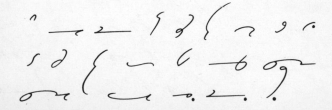

42. Brief-form derivatives ending in *s*.

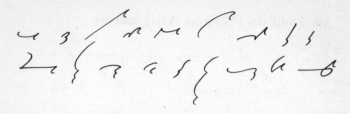

43. Reading Exercise

<small>A FAIRY TALE</small>

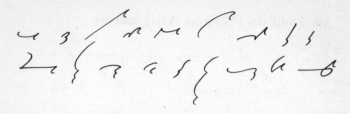

ASSIGNMENT 9

44. Drill on Previous Assignments

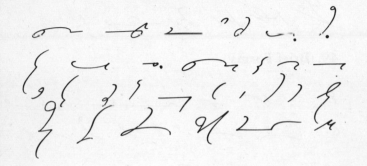

45. The letter *x* is usually expressed by an *s*, slightly modified in slant.

46. The suffix *tion* or *sion* is expressed by *sh*.

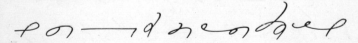

47. The past tense of abbreviated words is indicated by a disjoined *t*.

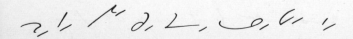

48. When the word is written in full, the past tense is joined, if possible.

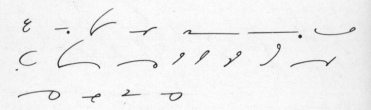

49. Brief Forms

50. Reading Exercise

TAXES

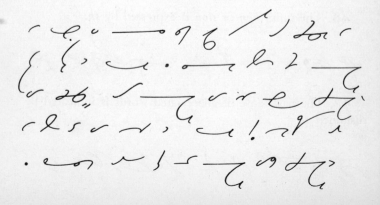

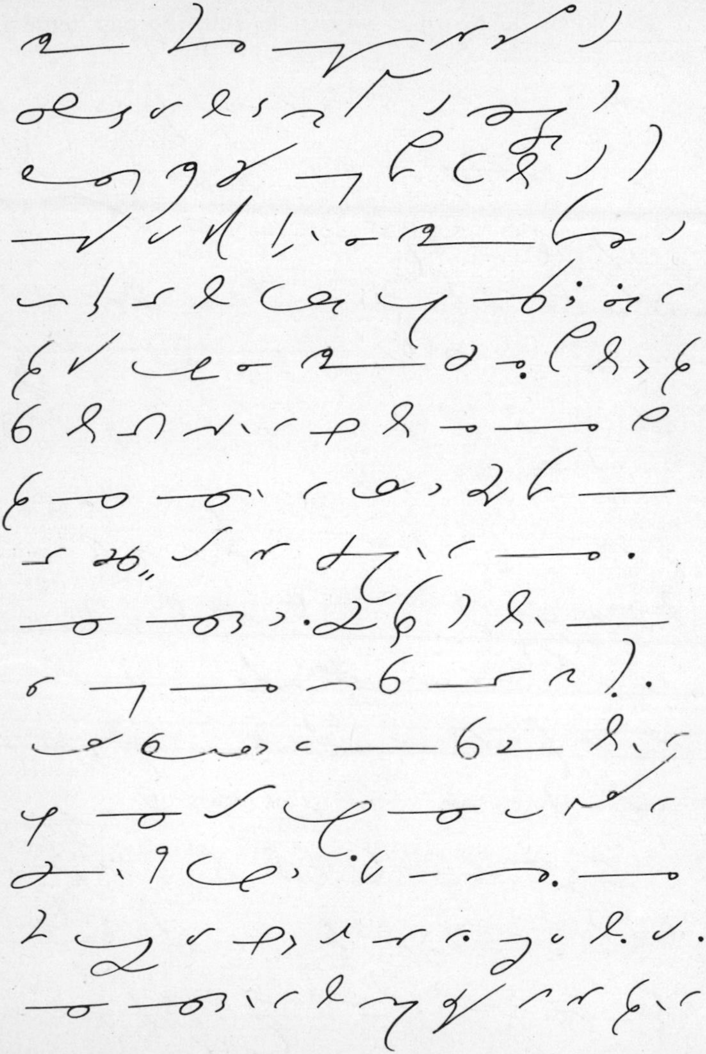

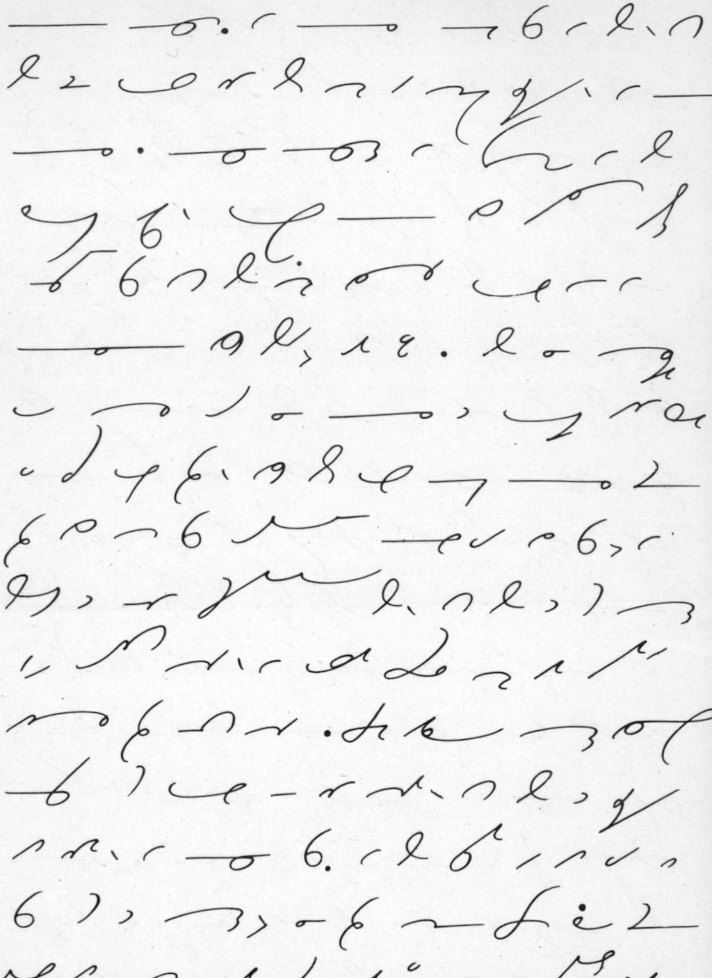

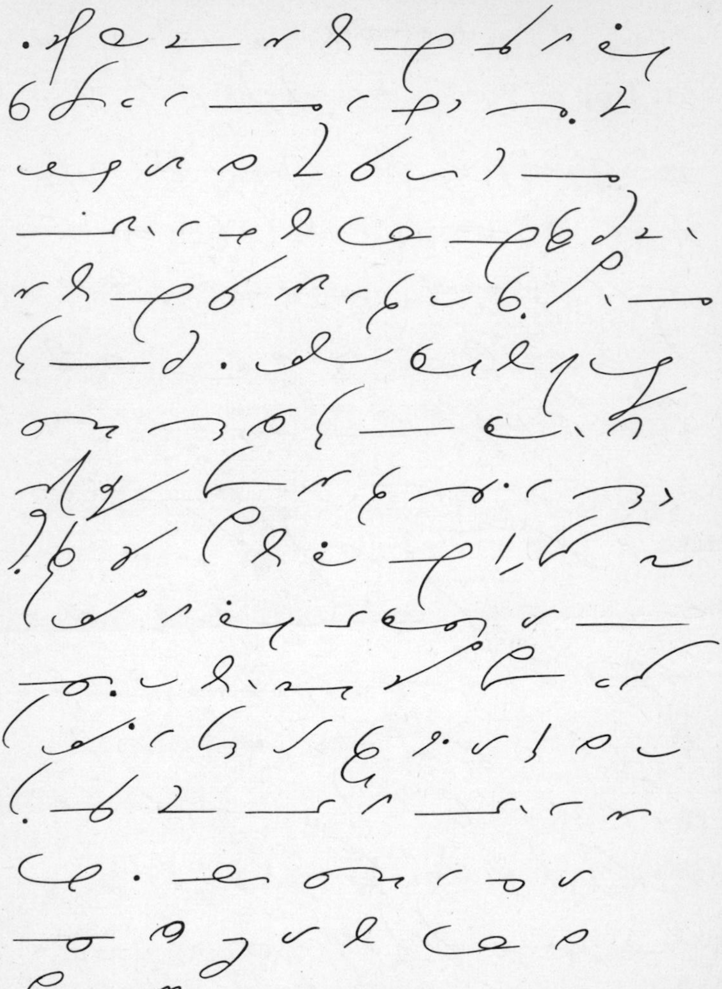

Assignment 10

51. Drill on Previous Assignments

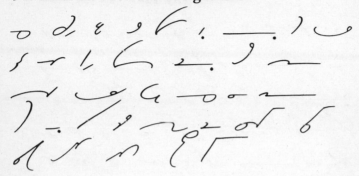

52. A brief form is sometimes used as part of another word.

53. Phrase Drill

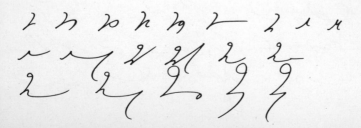

54. Reading Exercise

A LITTLE PIN

[Gregg shorthand outlines]

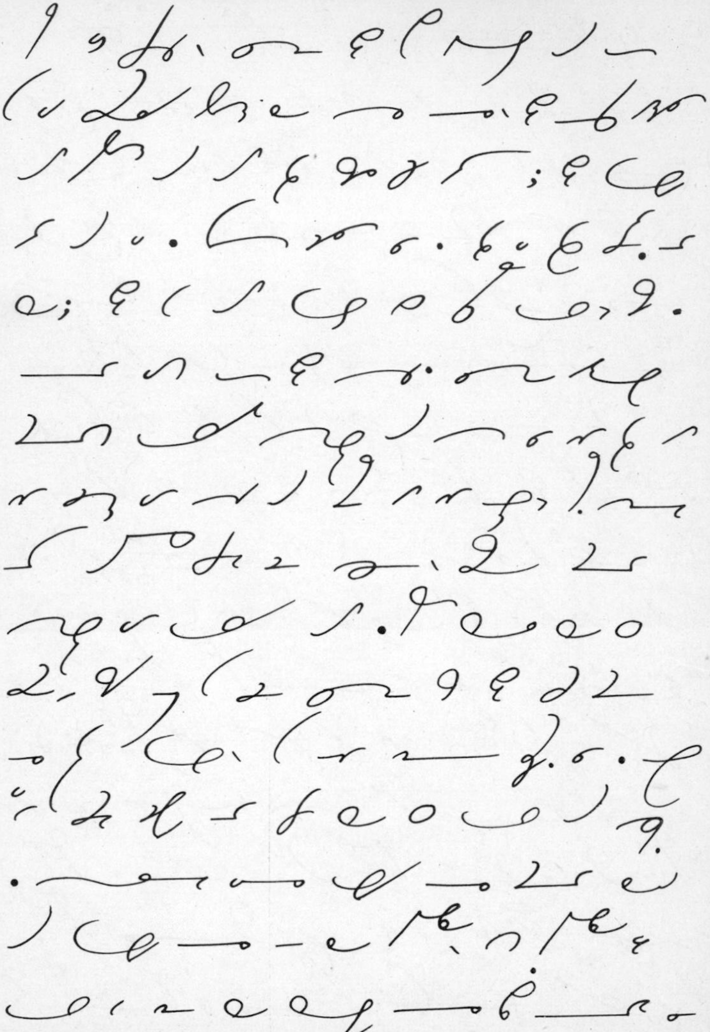

CHAPTER III

Assignment 11

55. Drill on Previous Assignments

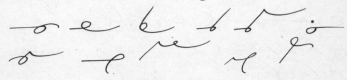

56. The lower half of the elliptical figure $\ominus$ is called the *o*-hook. It is used to express the following sounds:

ŏ	aw	ō
∪	∪̣	∪́
as in	*as in*	*as in*
rot	raw	wrote
∪	∪̣	∪́
r ŏ t	r aw	r ō t

57. The sound of *o* as in *no*.

54

58. The sound of *aw* as in *raw*.

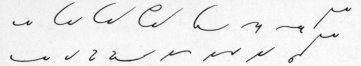

59. The sound of *o* as in *hot*.

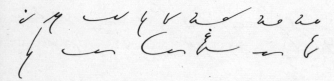

60. To avoid an angle, the hook may be turned on its side.

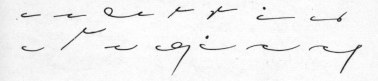

61. Reading Exercise

GLOBE TROTTING

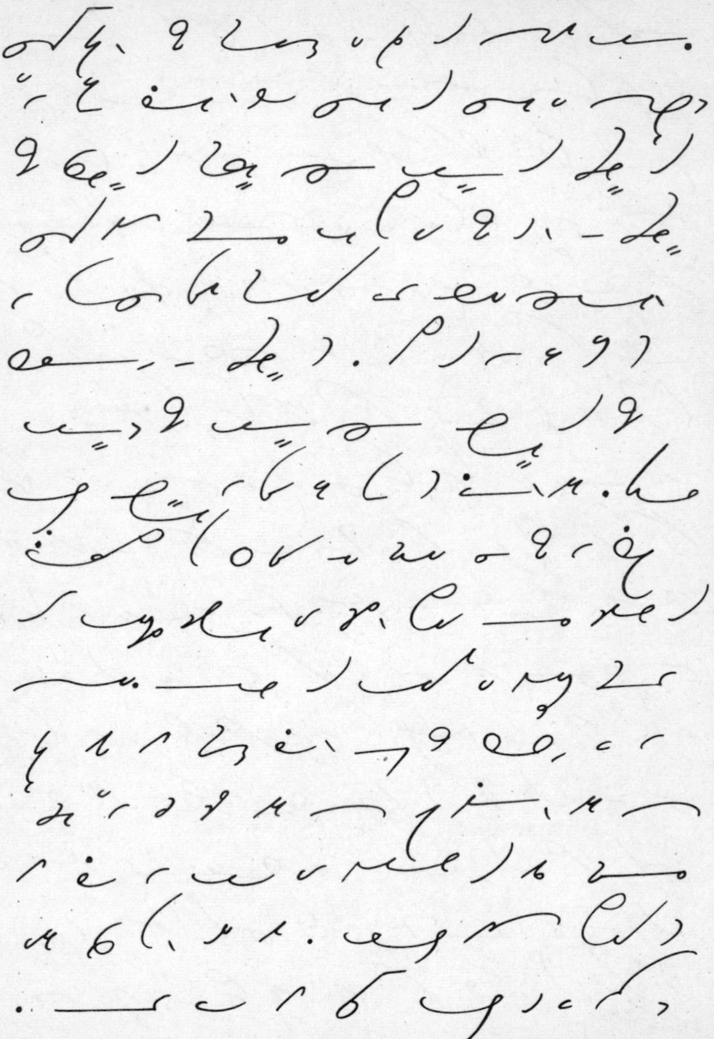

Assignment 12

62. Drill on Previous Assignments

[shorthand outlines]

63. Brief Forms

[shorthand outlines]

64. Brief-Form Derivatives

[shorthand outlines]

65. Phrase Drill

[shorthand outlines]

66. Reading Exercise

Hobbies

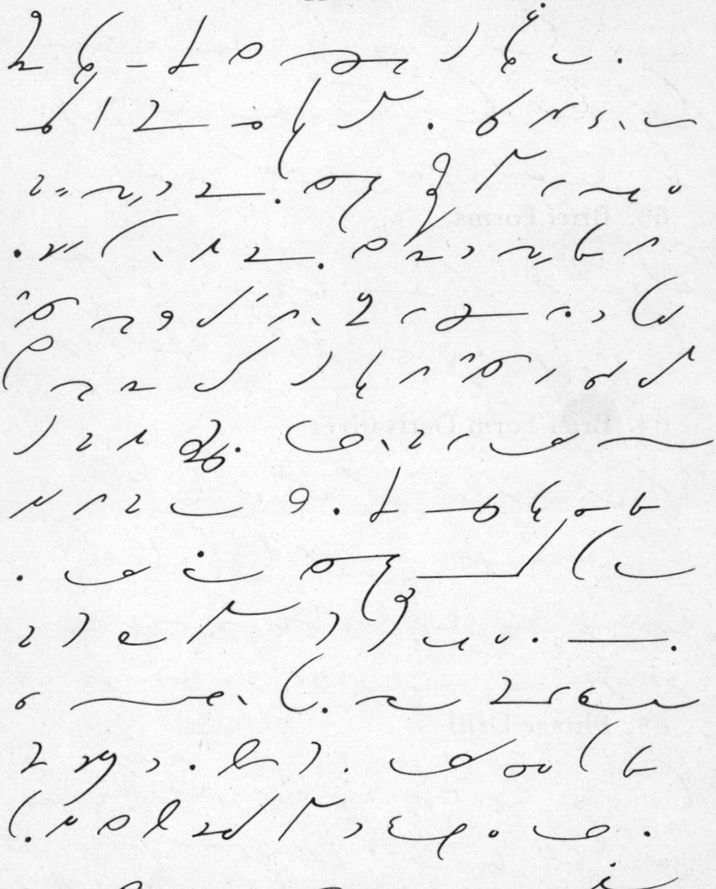

ASSIGNMENT 13

67. Drill on Previous Assignments

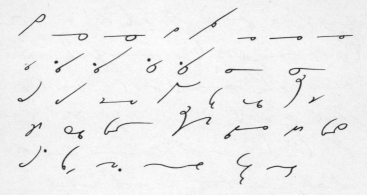

68. The letter *r* may often be expressed by writing the circle as though the *r* were to be written, and then simply omitting the *r*. The fact that the circle is written the other way on a straight line will indicate the presence of the *r*. For example:

69. Reading Exercise

The Honor of the Team

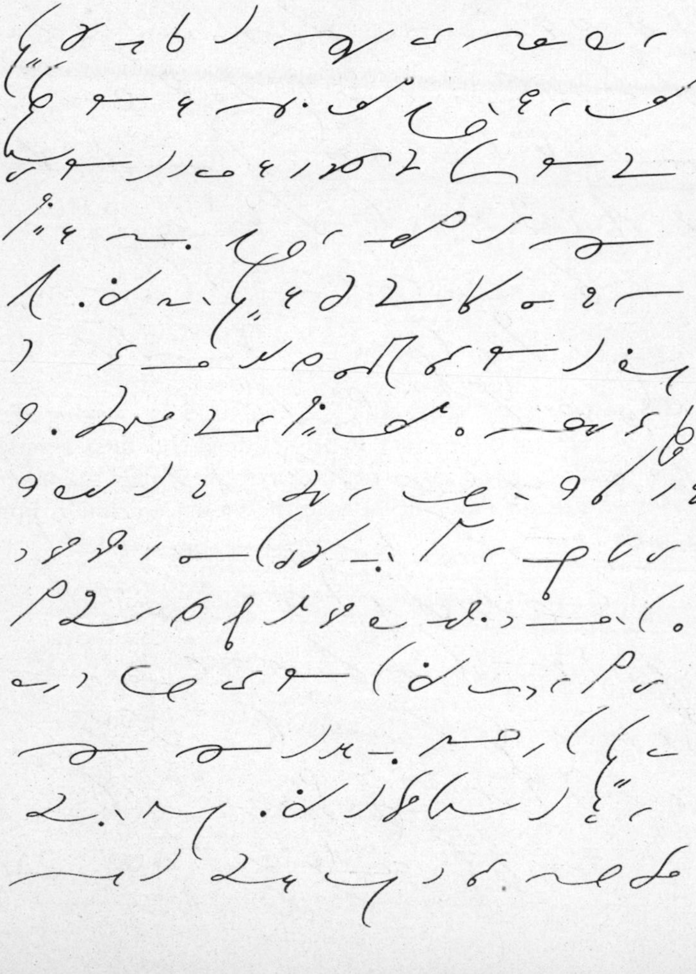

ASSIGNMENT 14

70. Drill on Previous Assignments

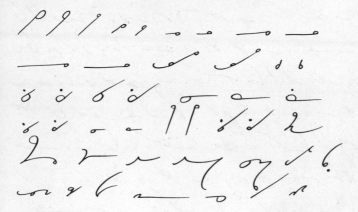

71. By changing the final circle to a loop, an *s* is added to such words as *dare*.

72. Brief Forms

73. Reading Exercise

A Hard Times Story

74-90 test next time

74. Drill on Previous Assignments

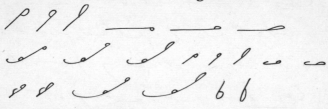

75. Two forms of *th* have been provided, to give an easy joining in any combination.

under "th" before o, l, r

76. The prefixes *con, com, coun,* followed by a consonant, are represented by *k.*

(a)

(b)

(c)

77. The suffix *ly* is expressed by a small circle; *ily* and *ally* by a loop.

(a)

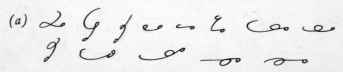

(b)   [shorthand outlines]

(c)   [shorthand outlines]

(d)   [shorthand outlines]

78. Reading Exercise

The Hermit

[shorthand outlines]

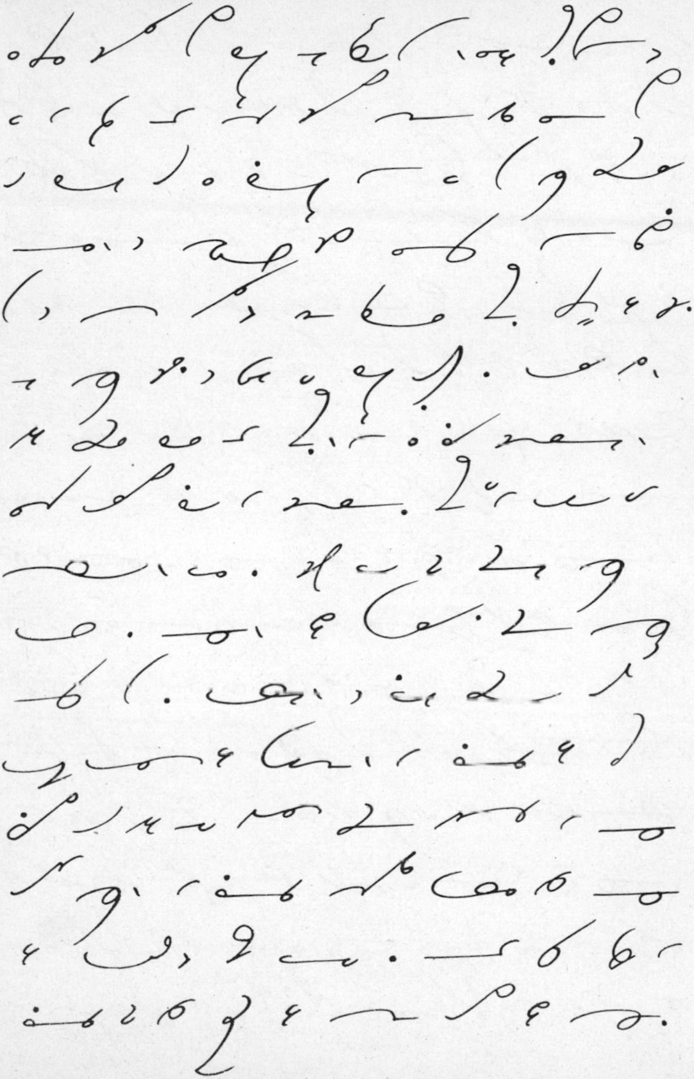

ASSIGNMENT 16

79. Drill on Previous Assignments

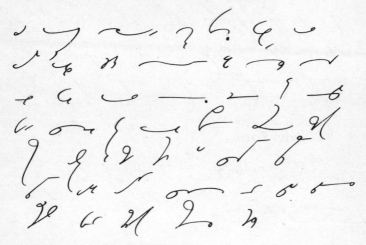

80. A Few Special Forms

81. In phrases, the word *to* is often expressed by *t*.

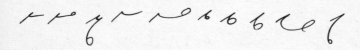

82. When repeated in a phrase, *as* is expressed by *s*.

83. After *be* or *been*, in phrases, the word *able* is expressed by *a*.

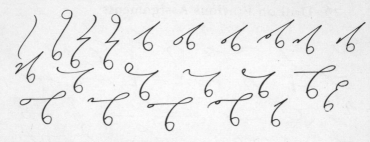

84. Brief Forms

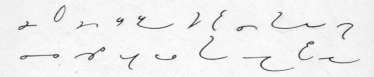

85. Reading Exercise

JOAN OF ARC

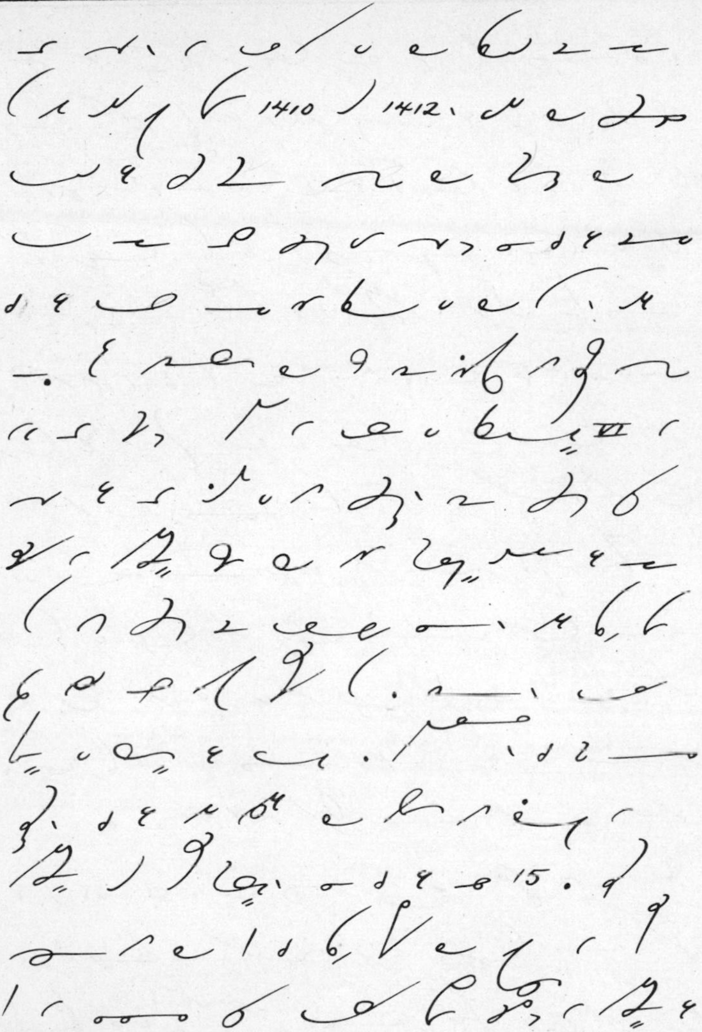
1410
1412
15

CHAPTER IV

ASSIGNMENT 17

86. Drill on Previous Assignments

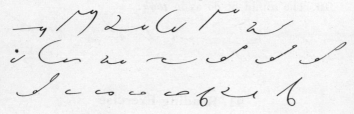

87. The upper part of the small elliptical figure ⟋ is called the *oo*-hook. It is used to express the following sounds:

ŭ	o͝o	o͞o
⌐	⌐	⌐
as in	*as in*	*as in*
tuck	took	tomb
⌐	⌐	⌐
t ŭ k	t o͝o k	t o͞o m

88. The sound of o͞o as in *who*.

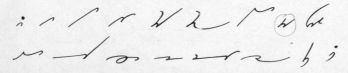

85

89. The sound of *ŭ* as in *cut*.

90. The sound of *ŏŏ* as in *took*.

91. Reading Exercise

A Secret Vacation

ASSIGNMENT 18

92. Drill on Previous Assignments

(shorthand outlines)

93. Brief Forms

(shorthand outlines)

94. Reading Exercise

PRAIRIE SOD MANSIONS

(shorthand outlines)

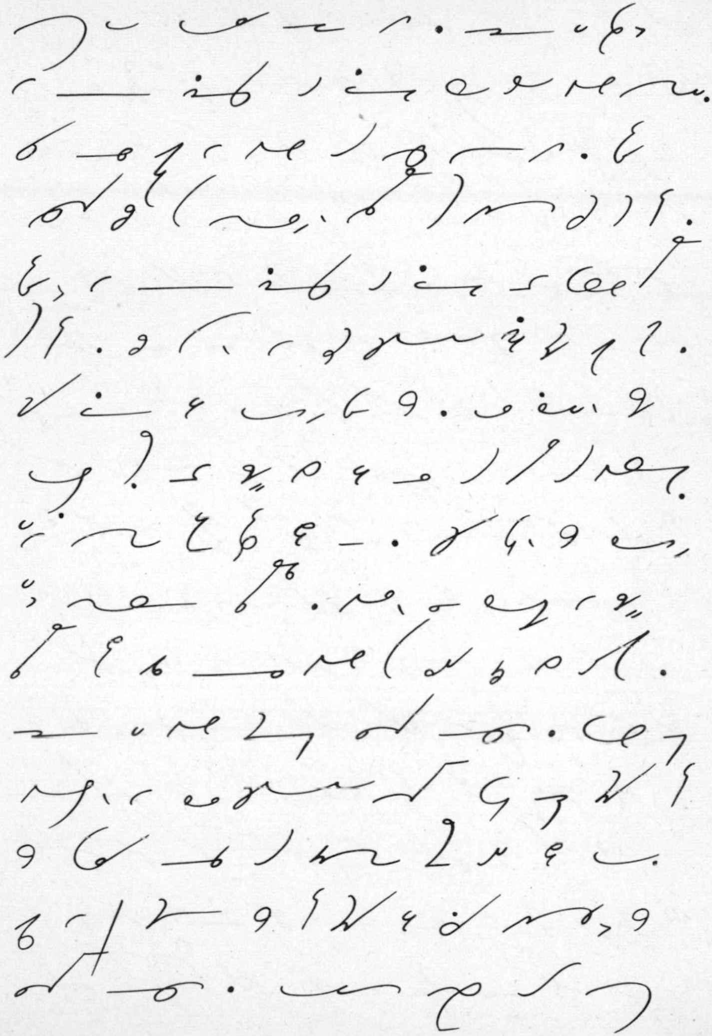

ASSIGNMENT 19

95. Drill on Previous Assignments

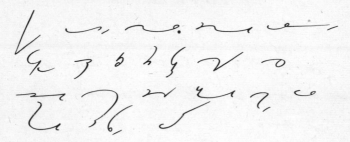

96.

X **96.** The sound of *w* at the beginning of words is represented by the *oo*-hook. The hook is also used in words beginning with *sw*.

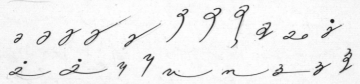

97. In the body of a word, it is more convenient to express the *w* by a dash placed beneath the vowel.

98. Words beginning *aw* or *ah* followed by a vowel.

99. Reading Exercise

A Day to Remember

(shorthand outlines)

ASSIGNMENT 20

100. Drill on Previous Assignments

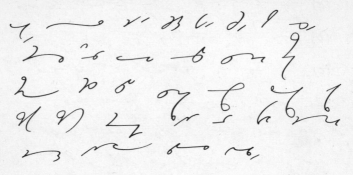

101. Brief Forms

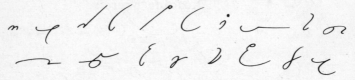

102. The sound of *y* is expressed by the small circle; *ye* is expressed by a small loop; *ya* by a large loop.

103. *Ng* is written ⌣ and *nk* is written ⌣

104. The prefixes *un, in, en, em, im,* followed by a consonant.

(a)

(b)

(c)

(d)

(e)

105. Reading Exercise

A FABLE

Assignment 21

106. Drill on Previous Assignments

107. The prefix *ex*.

108. The endings *ings* and *ingly*.

(a)

(b)

109. Special Negative Forms

110. Brief Forms.

111. Reading Exercise

Furs

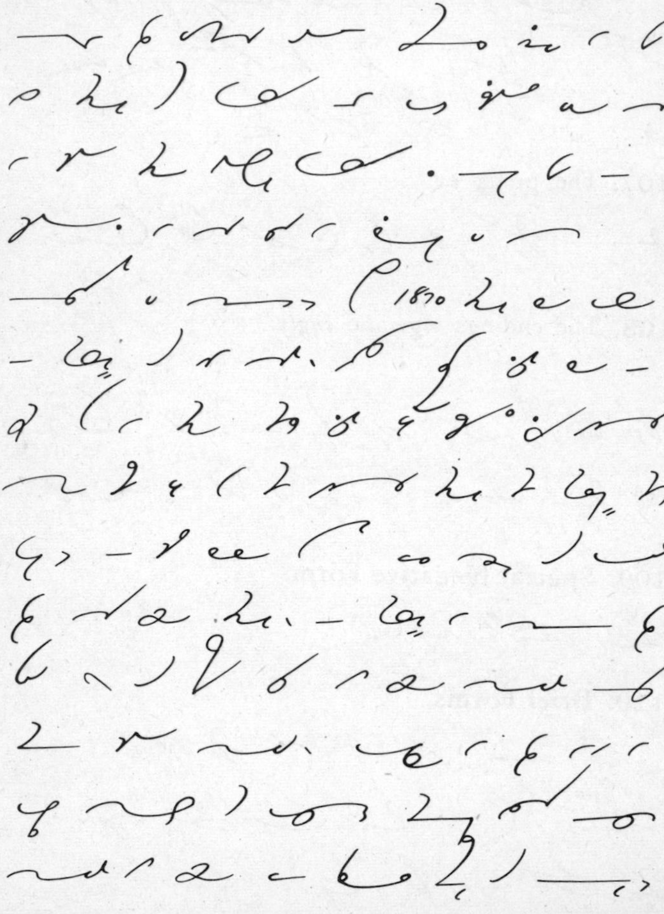

CHAPTER V

112. Drill on Previous Assignments

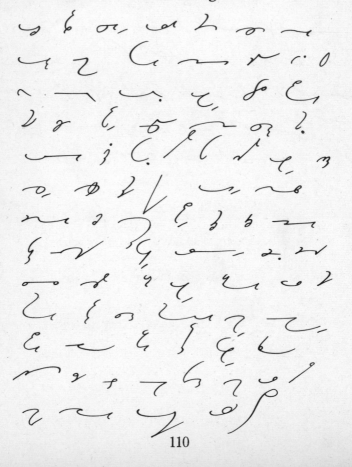

113. The diphthong *u* is written

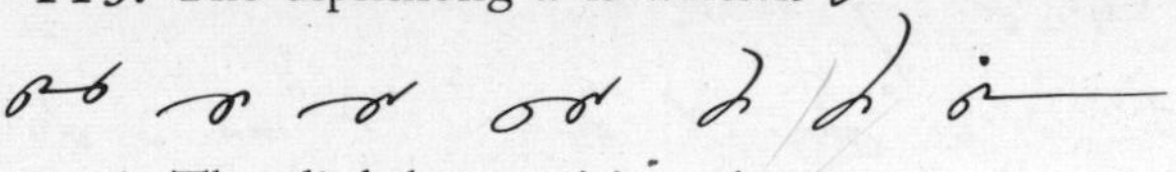

114. The diphthong *oi* is written

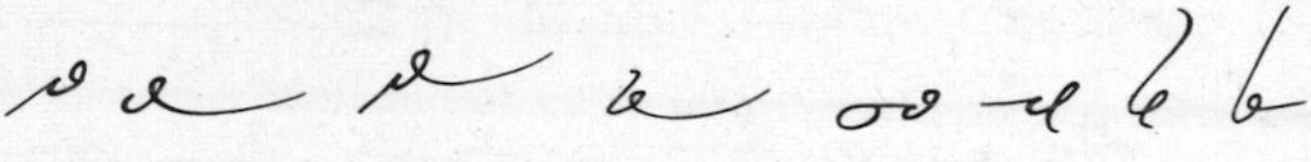

115. The dipthong *i* is written

116. The diphthong *ow* is written

117. Reading and Writing Exercise

A Toy Store

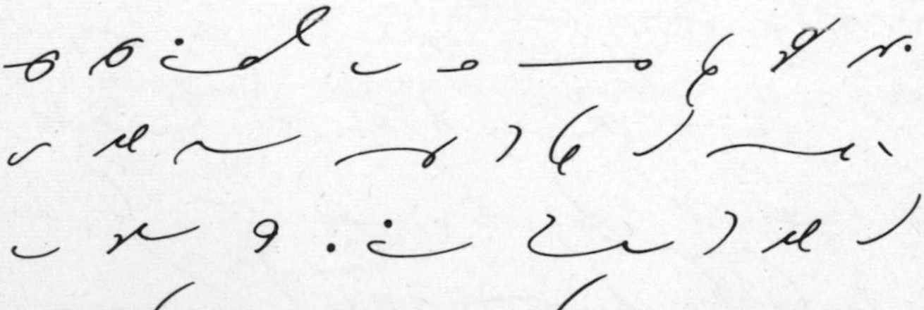

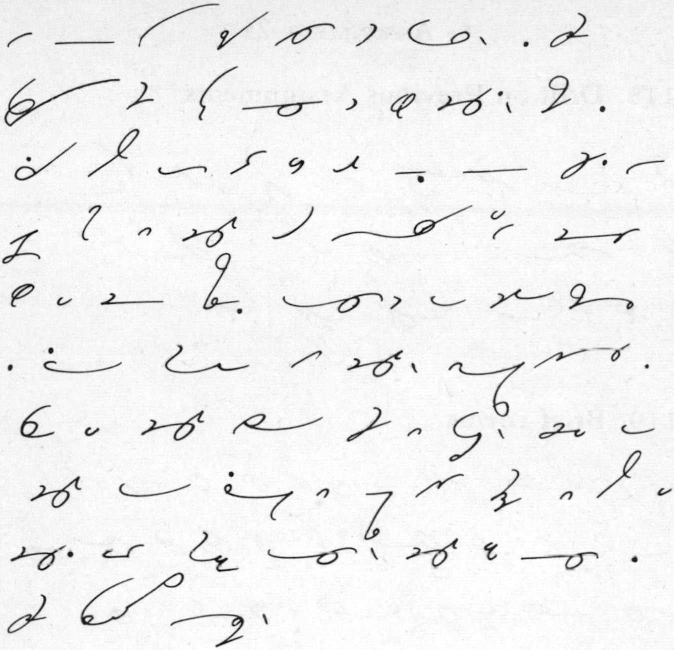

ASSIGNMENT 23

118. Drill on Previous Assignments

119. Brief Forms.

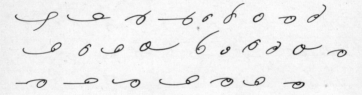

120. Reading and Writing Exercise

GREECE

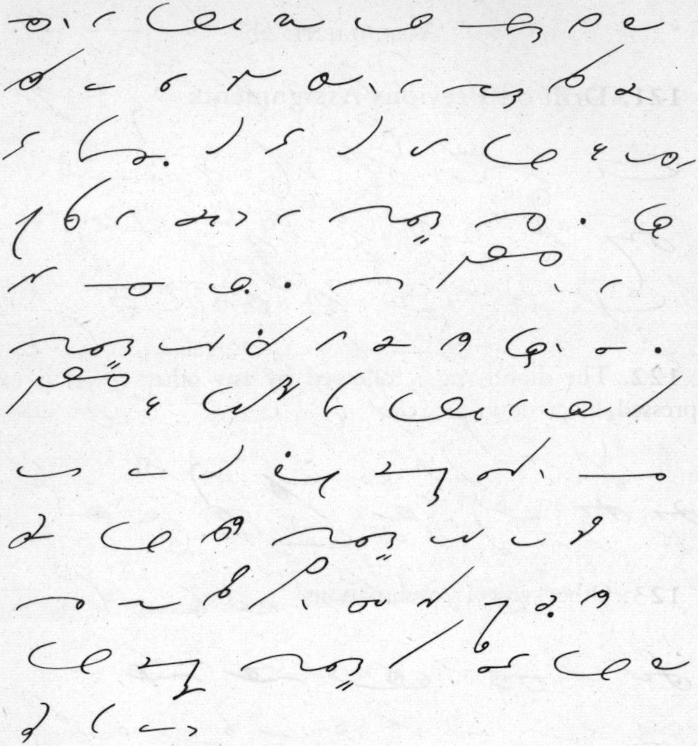

121. Drill on Previous Assignments

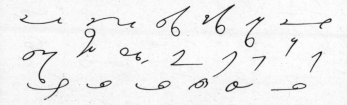

122. The diphthong *i* followed by any other vowel is expressed by a double circle.

123. Other vowel combinations.

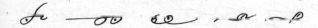

124. One vowel may often be omitted from a vowel combination. It is sometimes possible to express the diphthong *u* by the *oo*-hook—as it is often pronounced.

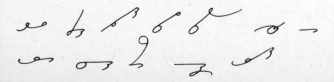

125. Brief Forms

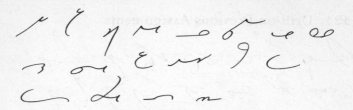

126. Reading and Writing Exercise

MONEY

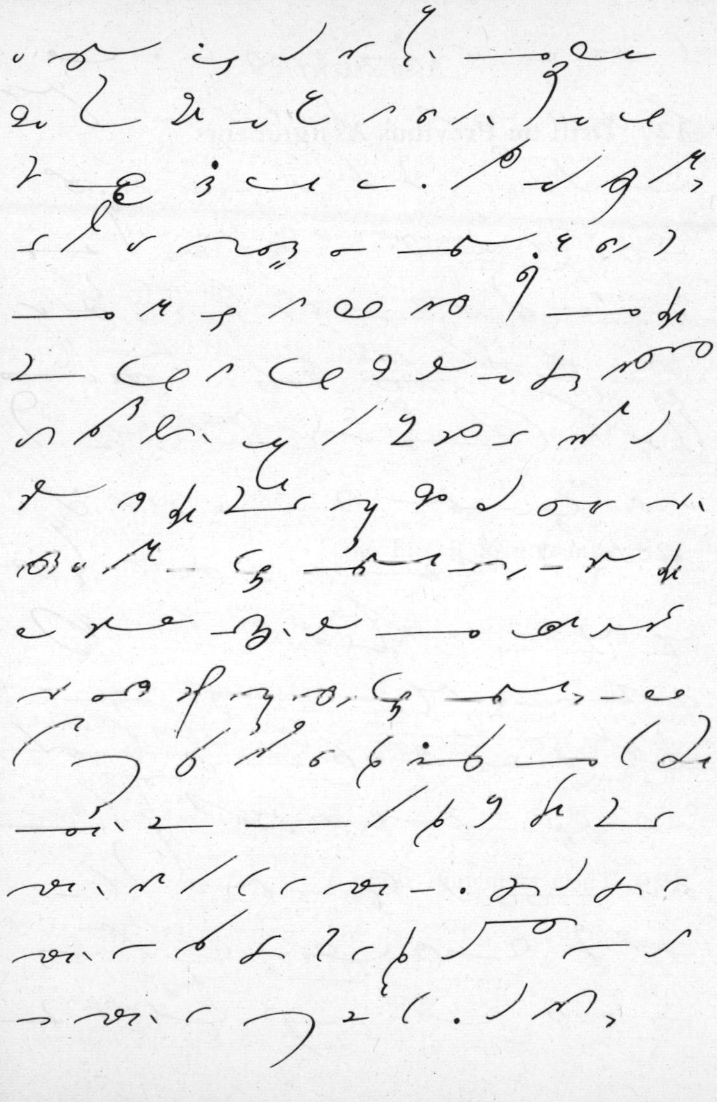

ASSIGNMENT 25

127. Drill on Previous Assignments

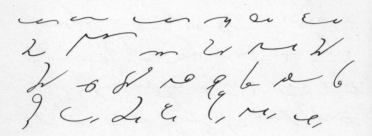

128. Omission of ŭ and *ow*.

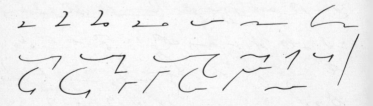

129. The termination *sume*.

130. Reading and Writing Exercise

Norway

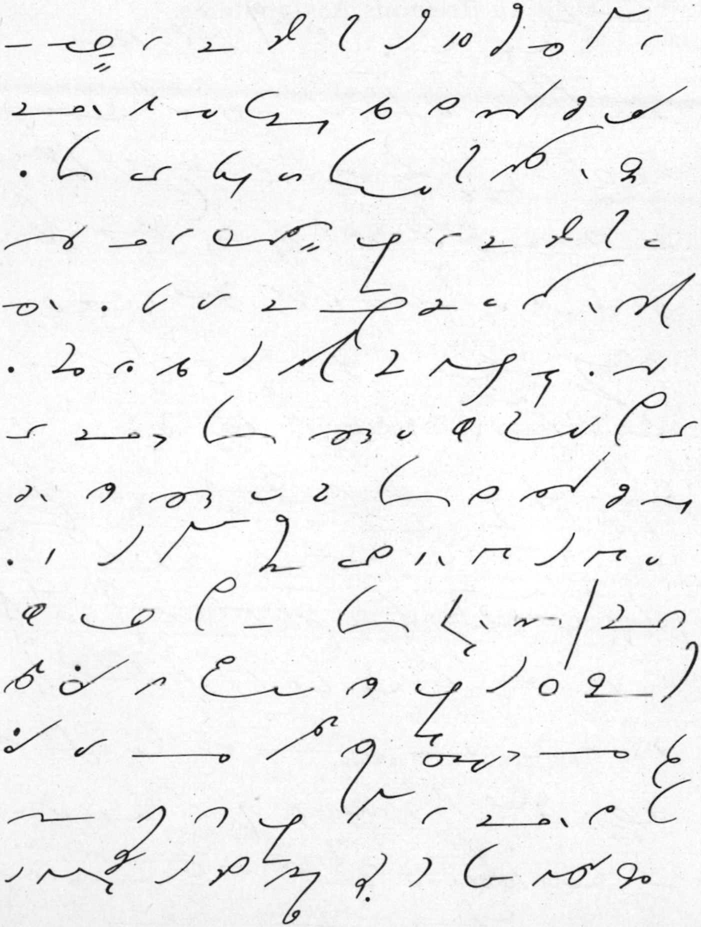

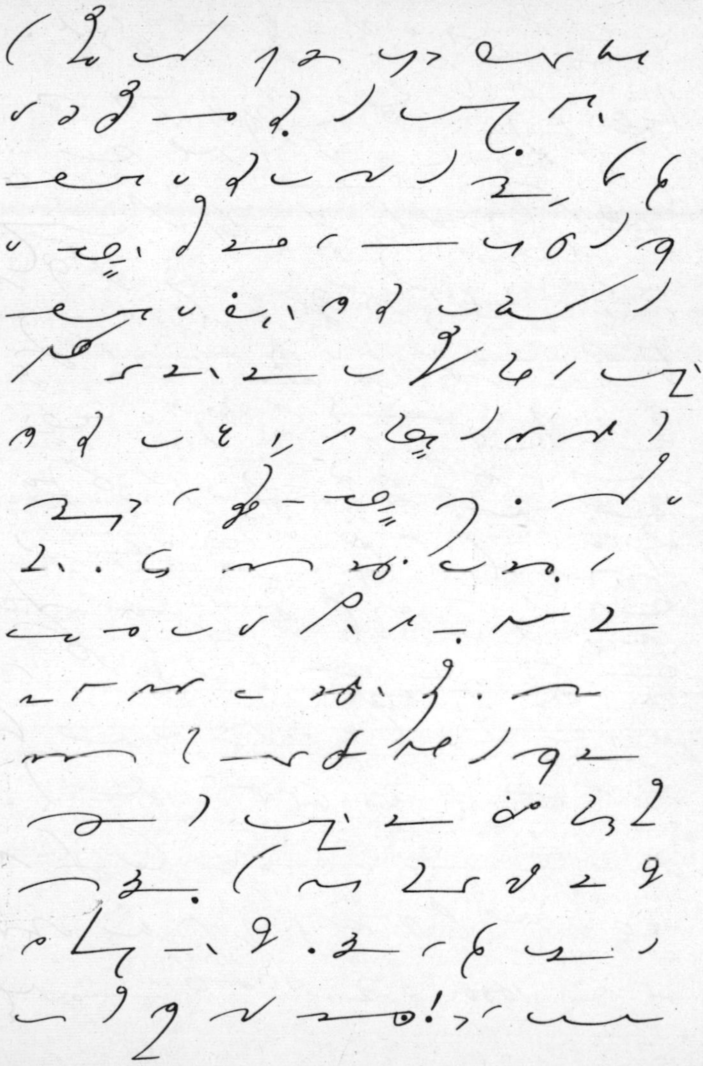

GREGG SHORTHAND

Ea. word 3 times

ASSIGNMENT 26

131. Drill on Previous Assignments

132. The syllables *per* and *pro*.

(a)

(b)

133. The termination *ble*.

134. The termination *ple*.

To be timed

135. Reading and Writing Exercise

The Power of a Smile

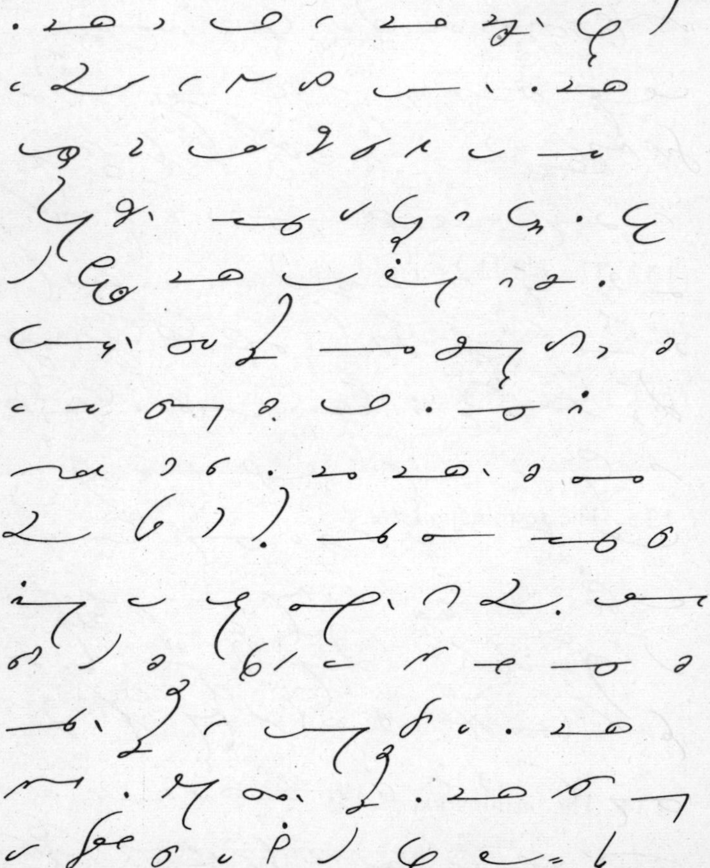

(shorthand outlines)

wds 3 *

136. Drill on Previous Assignments

137. The termination *ment*.

138. Brief Forms

139. Reading and Writing Exercise

The Man on Horseback

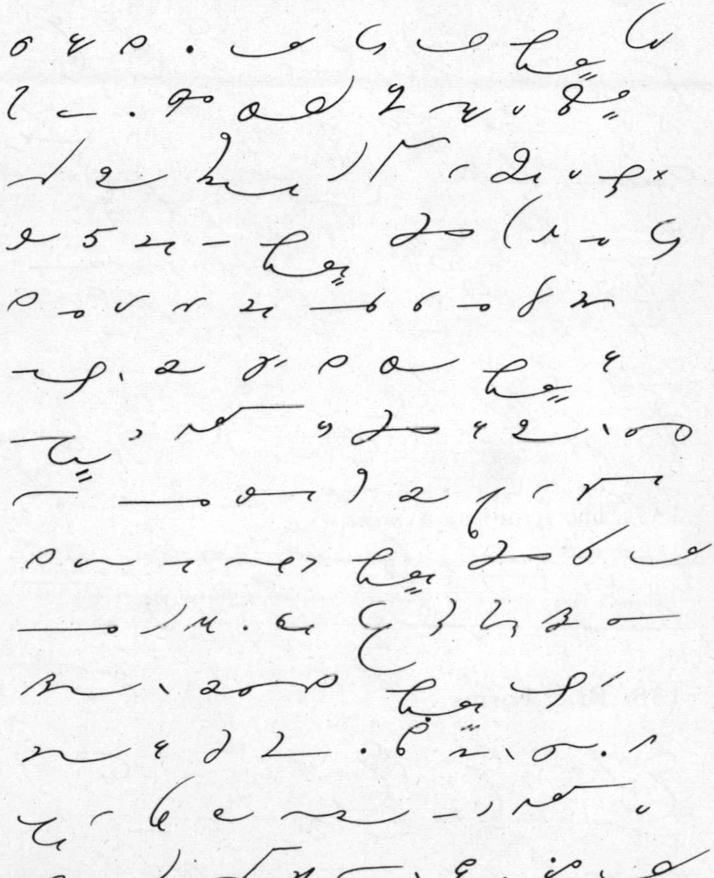

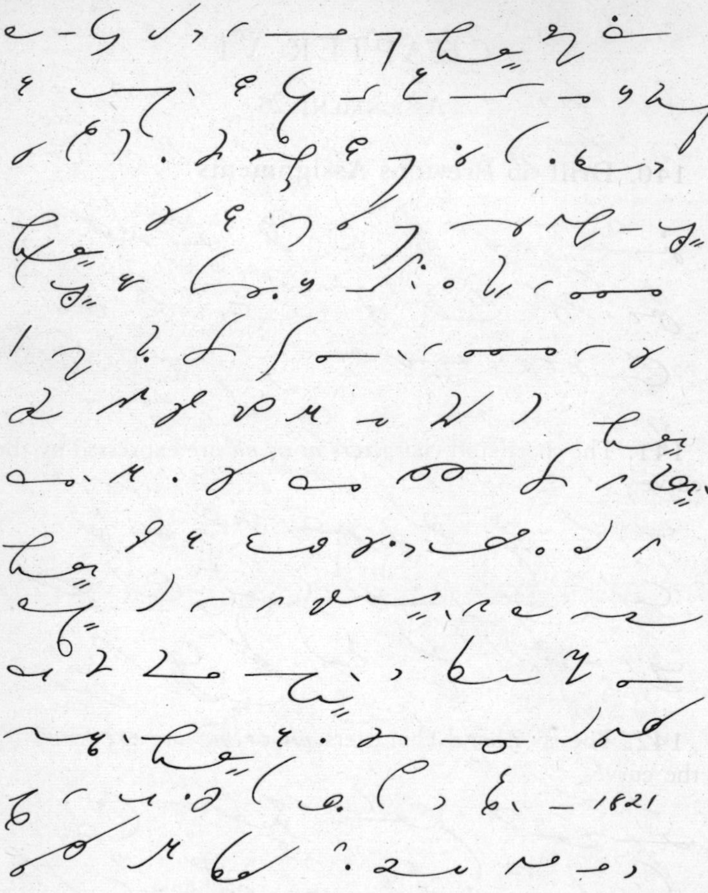
1821

CHAPTER VI

ASSIGNMENT 28

140. Drill on Previous Assignments

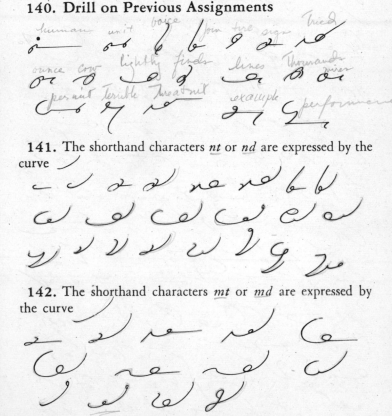

141. The shorthand characters *nt* or *nd* are expressed by the curve

142. The shorthand characters *mt* or *md* are expressed by the curve

143. Reading and Writing Exercise

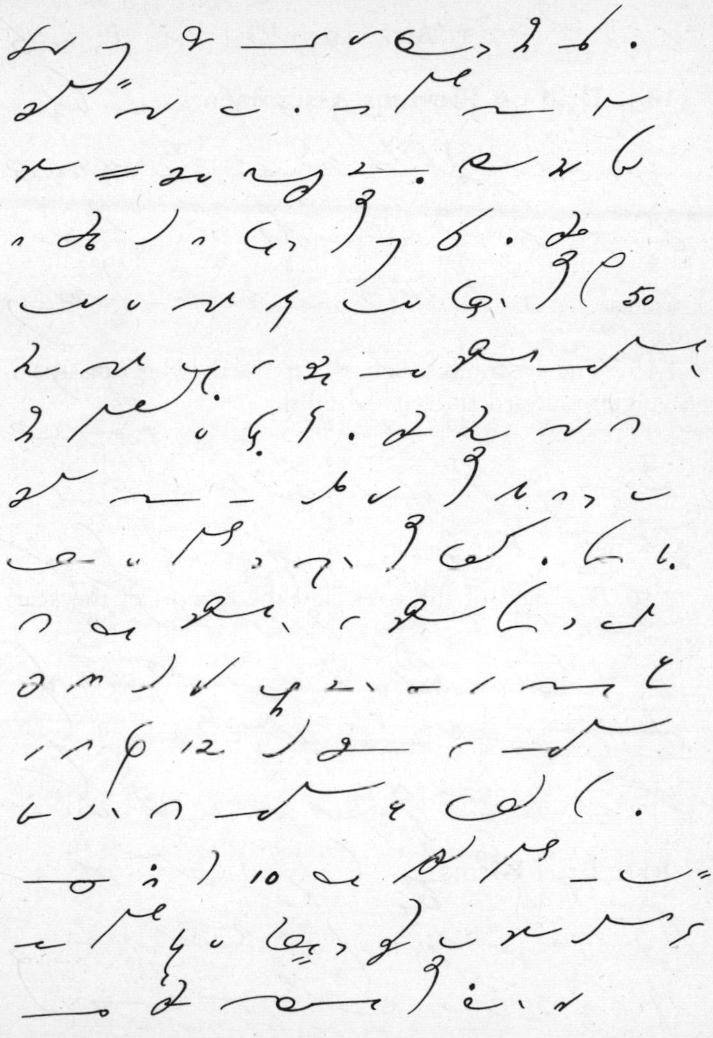

ASSIGNMENT 29

144. Drill on Previous Assignments

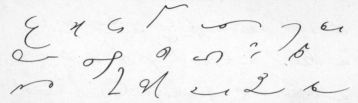

145. The *ld* combination is expressed by giving the *l* a swinging upward turn at the finish.

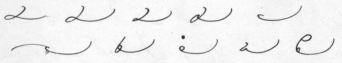

146. The days of the week and the months of the year.

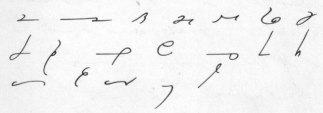

147. Brief Forms

148. Reading and Writing Exercise

A BIRTHDAY PARTY

[Gregg shorthand outlines]

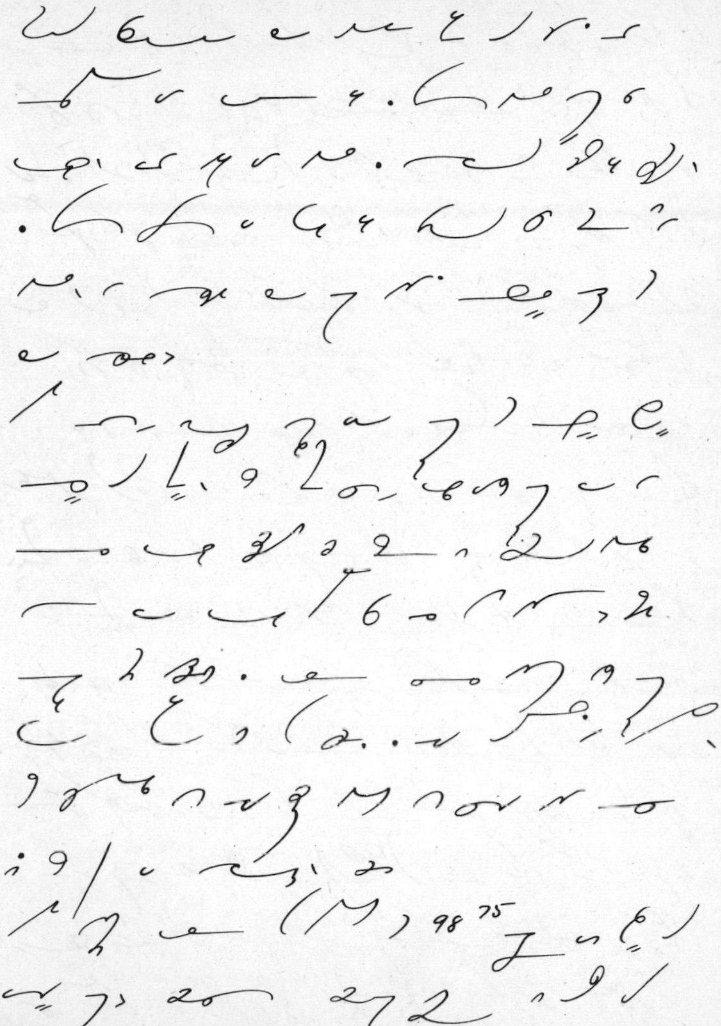

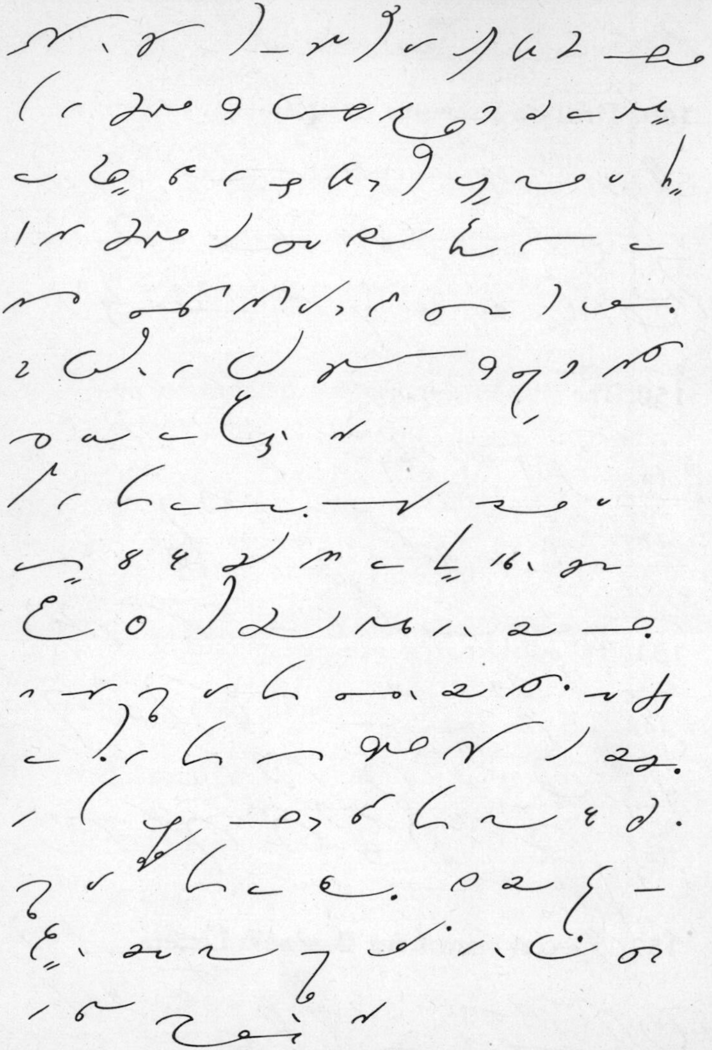

ASSIGNMENT 30

write out

149. Drill on Previous Assignments

[shorthand outlines]

✔ **150.** The syllables *jent-d, pent-d* are expressed by ∪

(a) *[shorthand outlines]*

(b) *[shorthand outlines]*

✔ **151.** The syllables *def-v, tive* are expressed by ∩

(a) *[shorthand outlines]*

(b) *[shorthand outlines]*

(c) *[shorthand outlines]*

152. Special Forms for Business Letters

153. Reading and Writing Exercise

JOHN SMITH AND THE NEW WORLD

reading speed test.

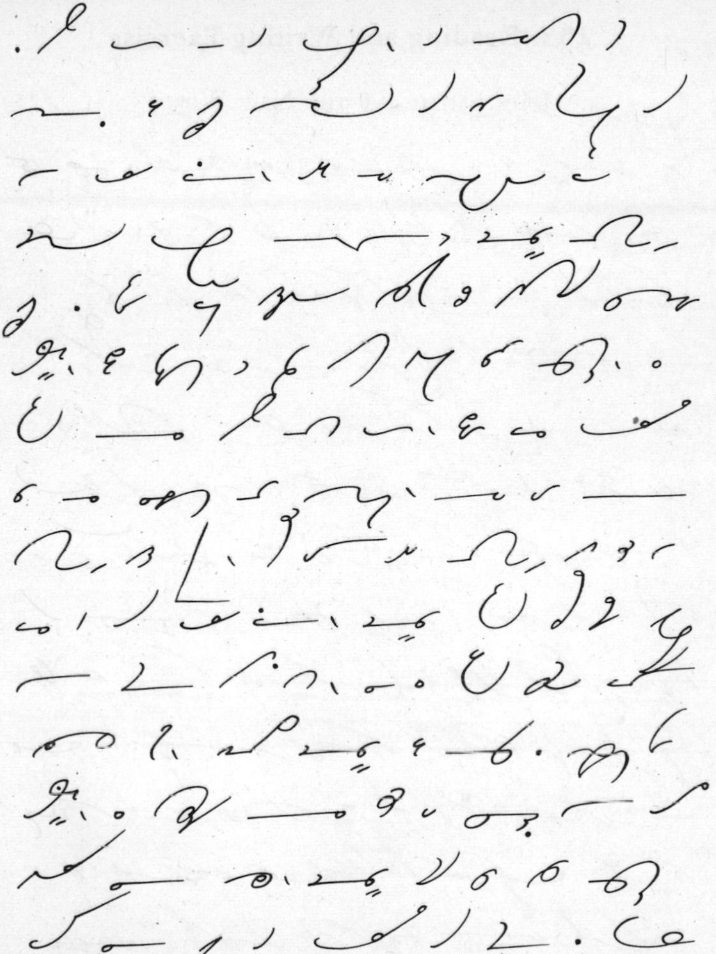

Assignment 31

154. Drill on Previous Assignments

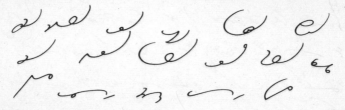

155. Brief Forms

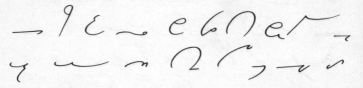

156. Reading and Writing Exercise

Robin Hood and His Merry Men

(shorthand outlines)

ite
times

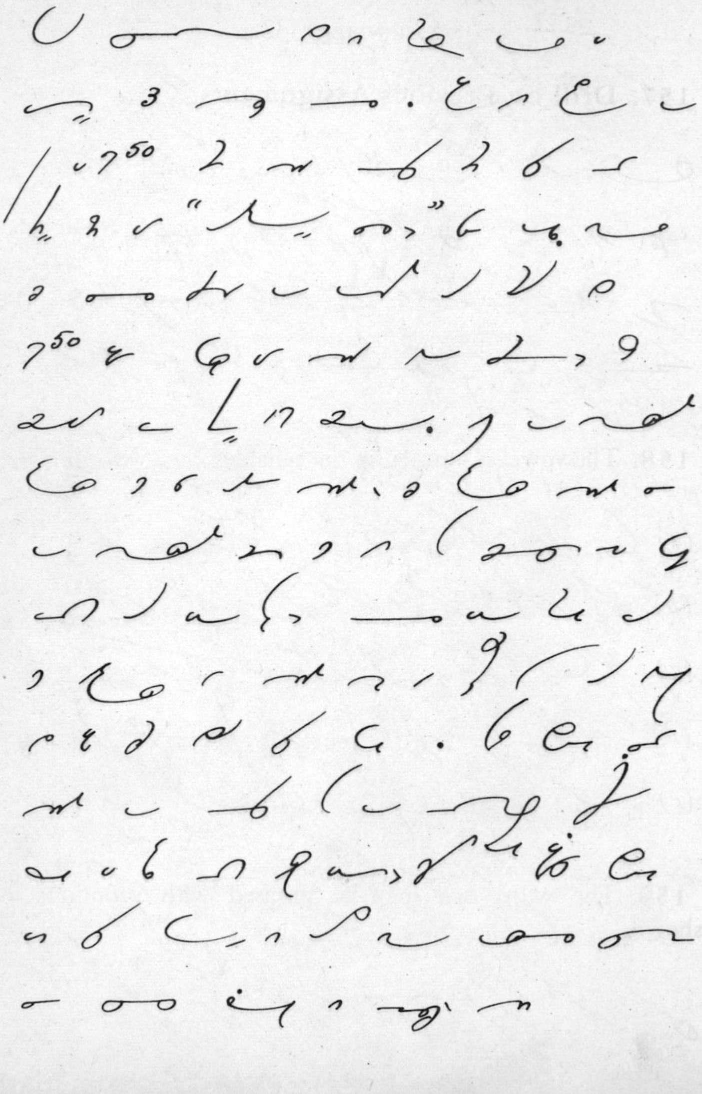

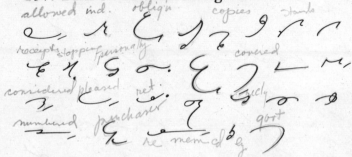

✓ ASSIGNMENT 32

157. Drill on Previous Assignments

158. The vowel is omitted in the syllables *be, de, dis, mis, re.*

(a)

(b)

(c)

(d)

(e)

159. The word *had* may be phrased with pronouns as shown.

160. Reading and Writing Exercise

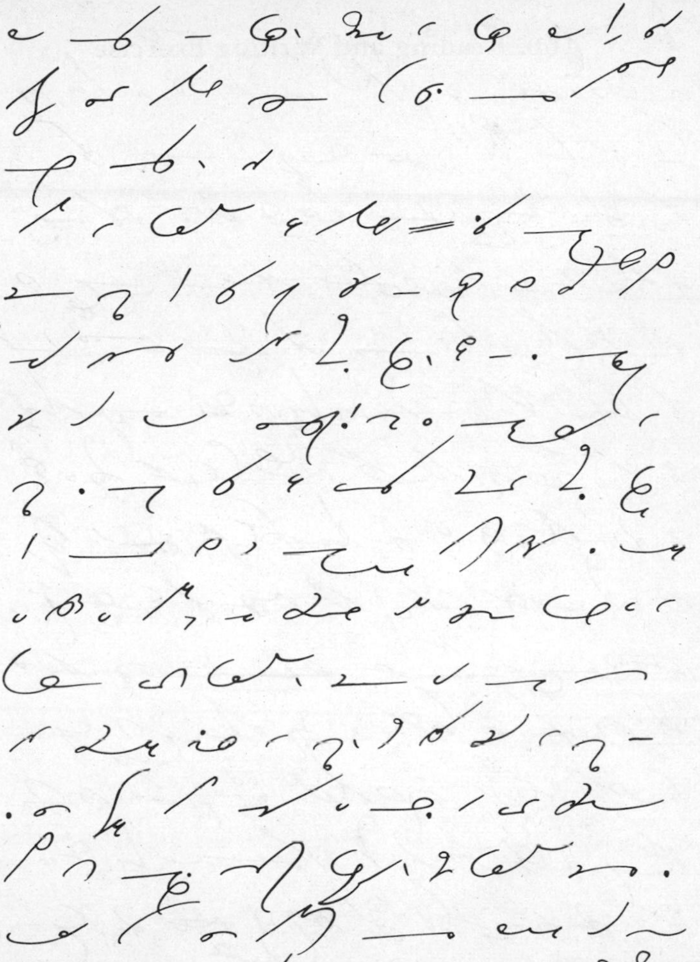

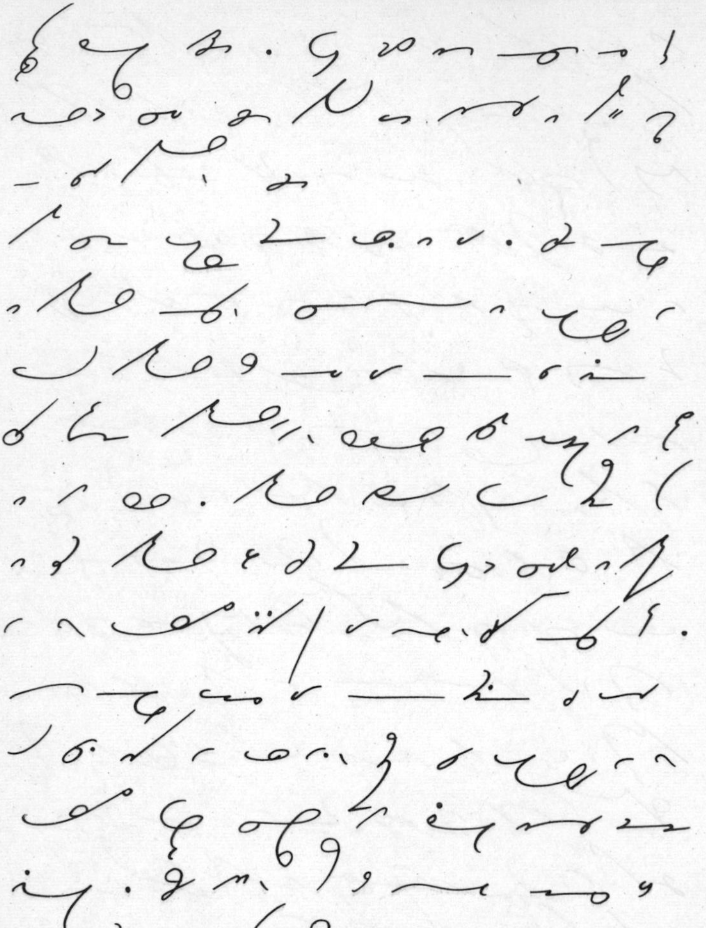

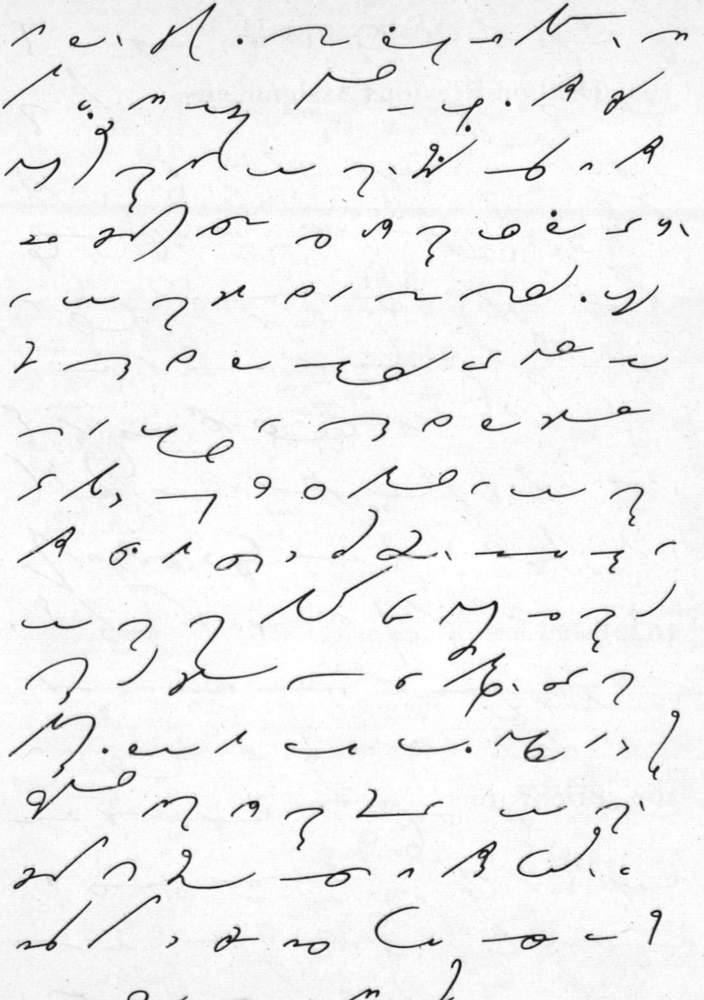

161. Drill on Previous Assignments

162. Forms for *was not* and *is not*.

163. Brief Forms

164. Reading and Writing Exercise

The Story of Printing

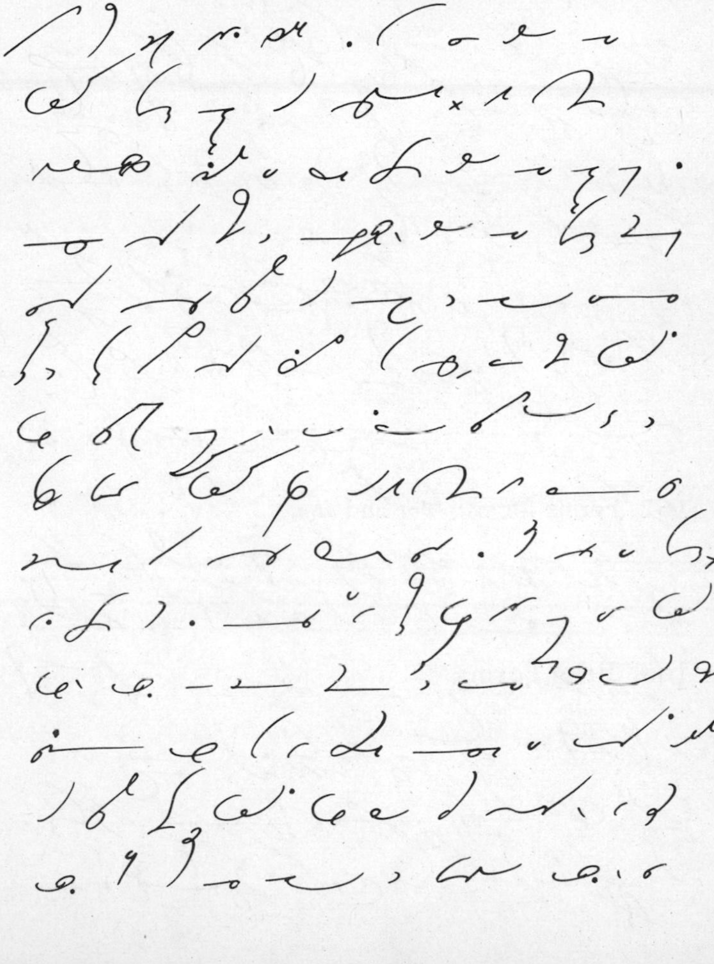

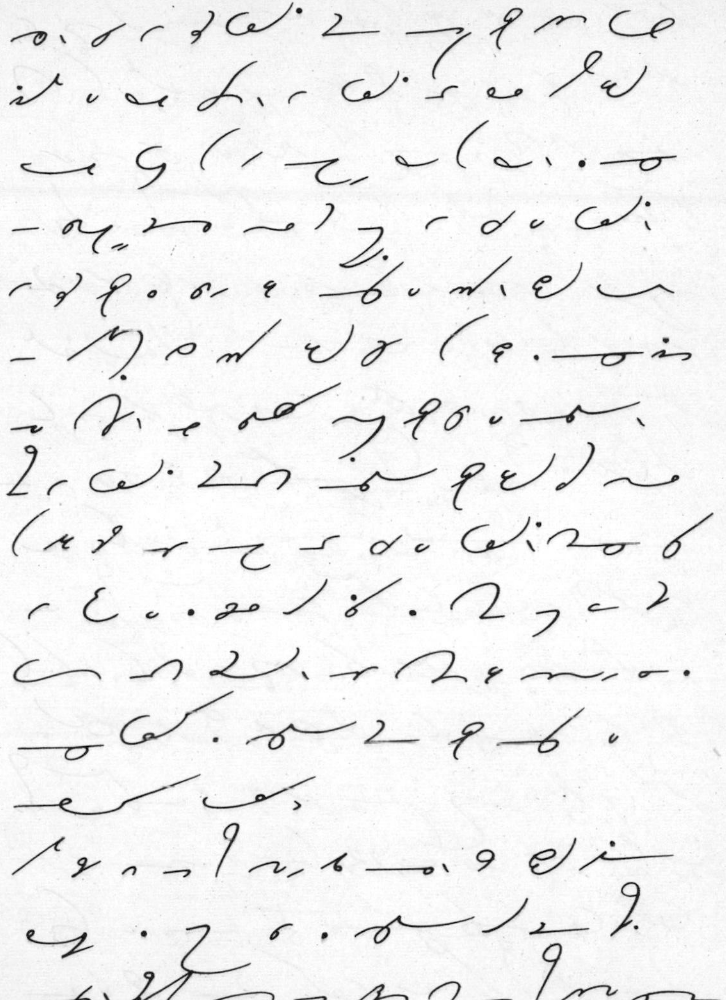

CHAPTER VII

write

165. Drill on Previous Assignments

166. The syllables *den, ten* are expressed by

(a)

(b)

167. The syllables *dem, tem* are expressed by

(a)

(b)

171

168. Phrase Drill

169. Reading and Writing Exercise

A FRIENDLY VISIT

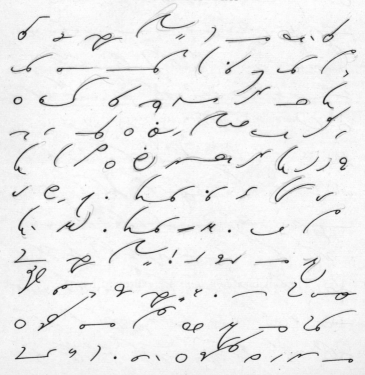

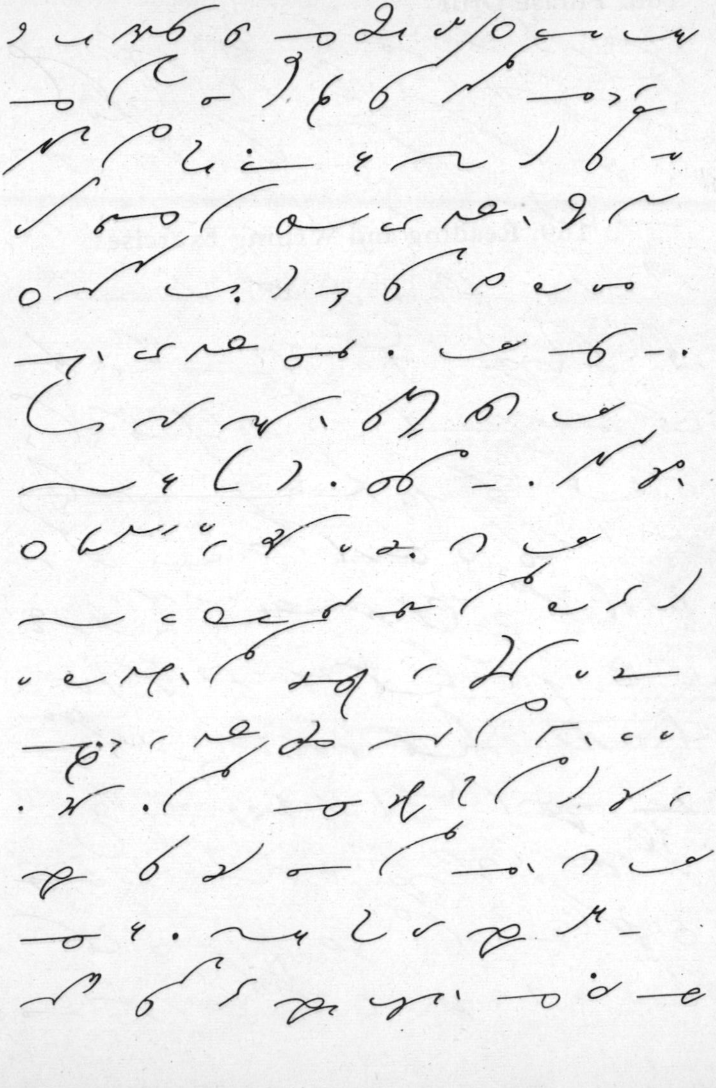

(shorthand outlines)

Write.

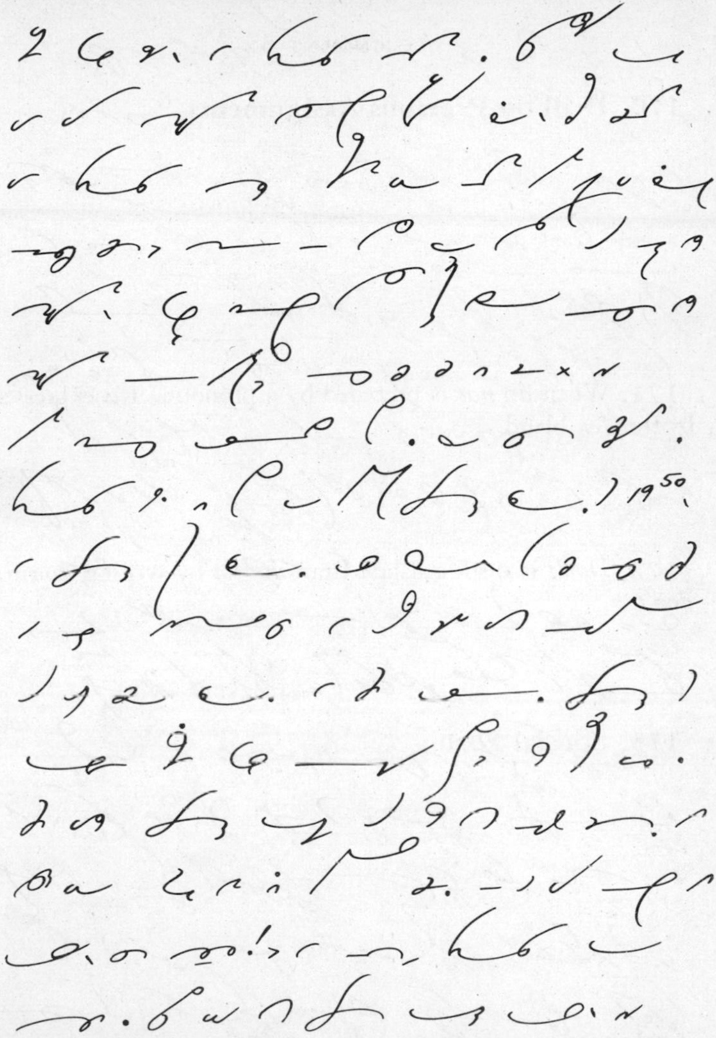

Do all letters Twice —

Assignment 35

170. Drill on Previous Assignments

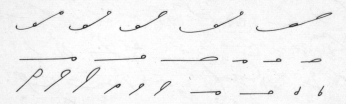

171. When *do not* is preceded by a pronoun, it is expressed by the *den* blend.

172. *Don't* is distinguished from *do not* by writing *don* for *don't*.

173. Special Forms

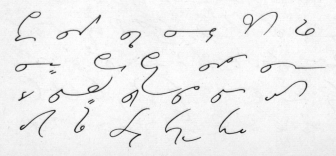

174. Reading and Writing Exercise

A Sacrifice

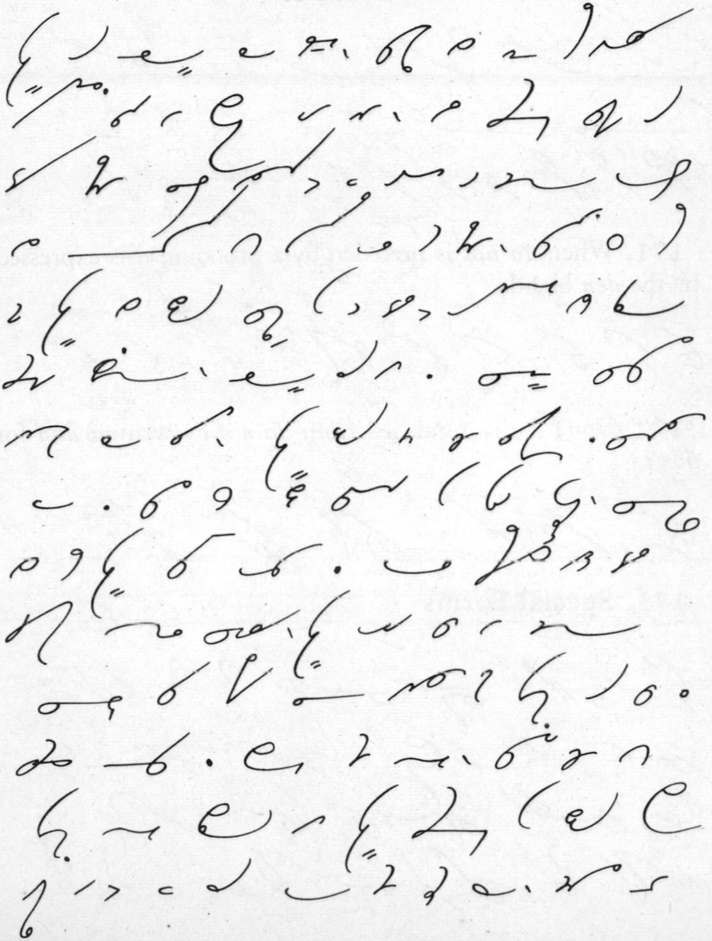

Assignment 36

175. Drill on Previous Assignments

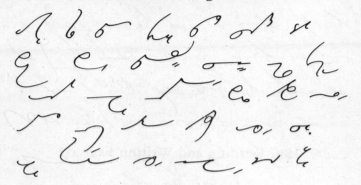

176. The indication of *r*.

177. The indication of *r*. *(Continued.)*

178. The indication of *r*. *(Continued.)*

179. The omission of *r*.

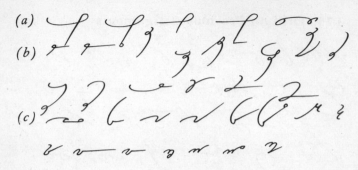

(a)

(b)

(c)

180. Reading and Writing Exercise

MOLLY PITCHER

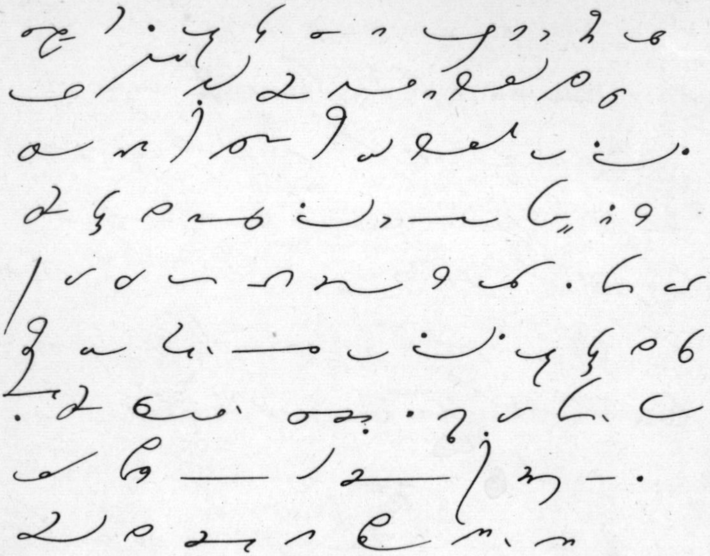

Assignment 37

181. Drill on Previous Assignments

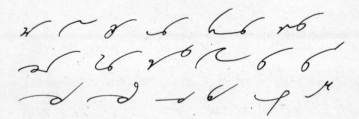

182. The syllables *tern*, *dern* are expressed by *ten*.

183. The syllable *ther* at the end of words.

184. Special Forms

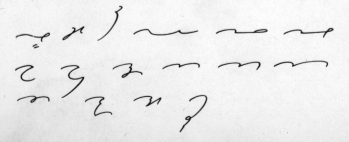

His 5-76

Write 2x

185. Reading and Writing Exercise

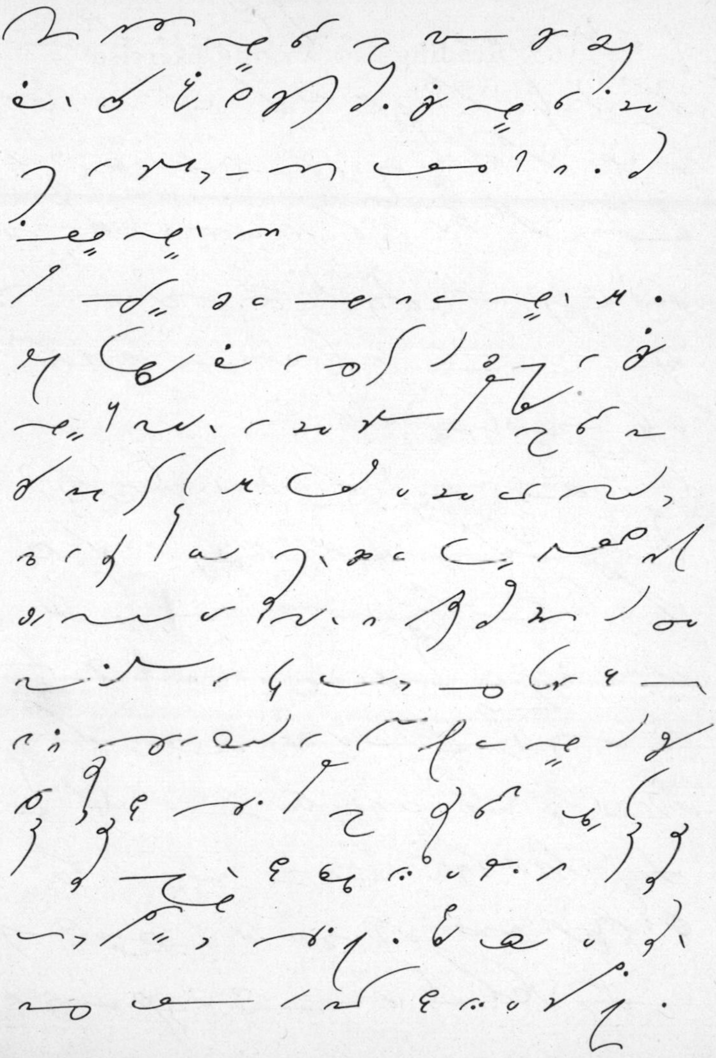

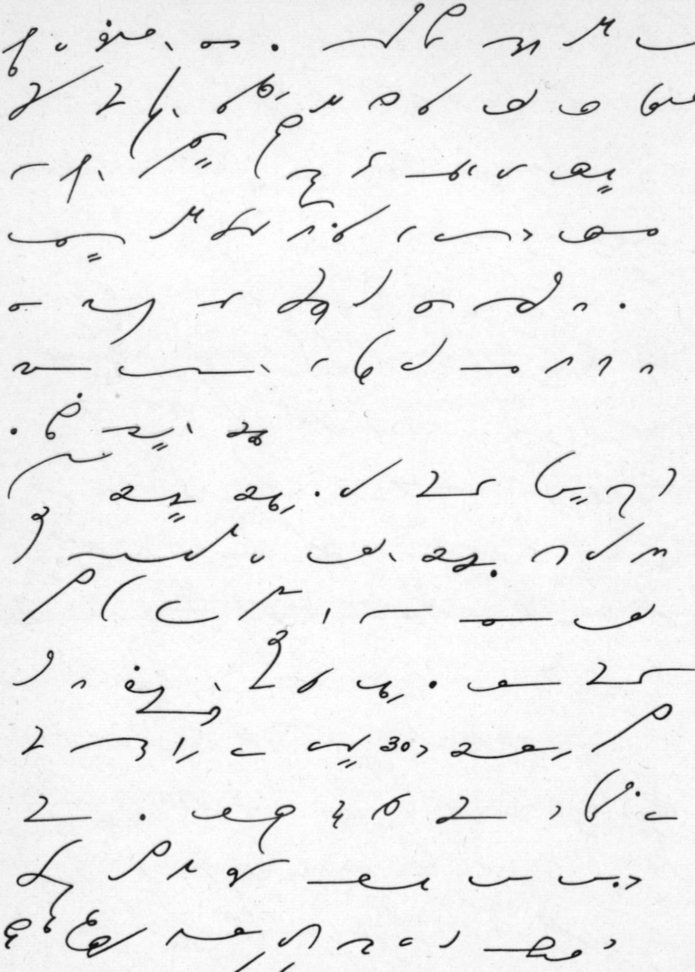

ASSIGNMENT 38

186. Drill on Previous Assignments

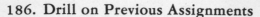

187. The prefixes *for, fore, fur.*

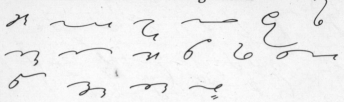

188. The endings *ify* and *full.*

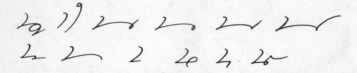

189. The endings *self* and *selves.*

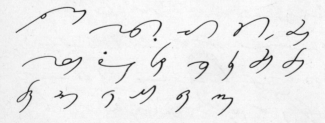

190. The ending *age.*

191. Reading and Writing Exercise

THE FURNACE

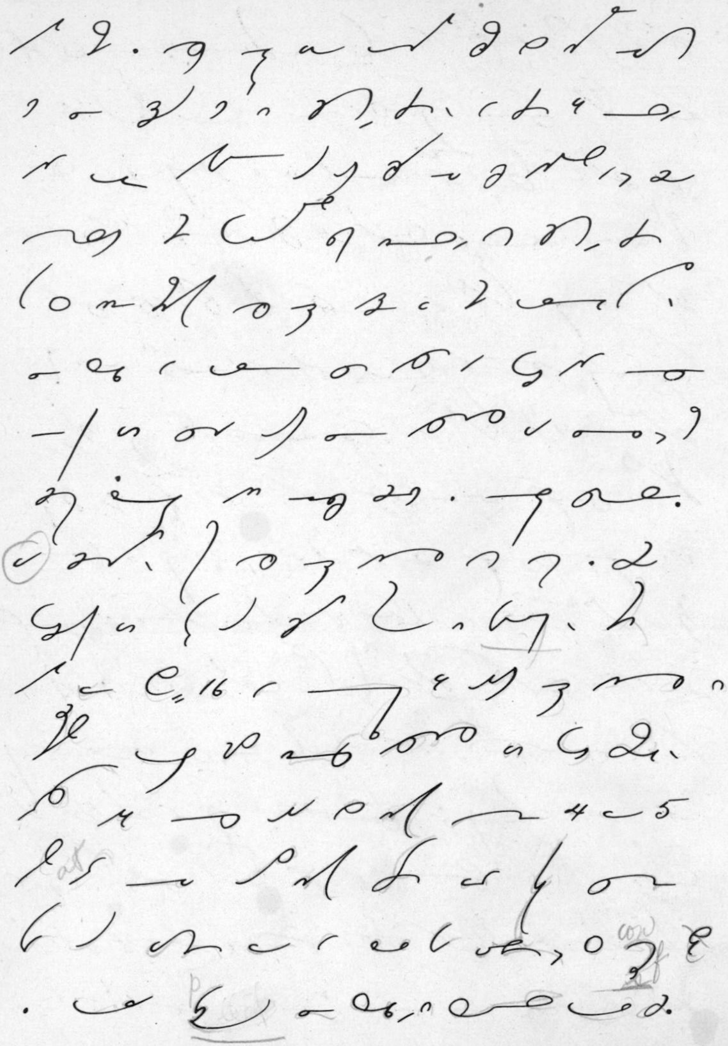

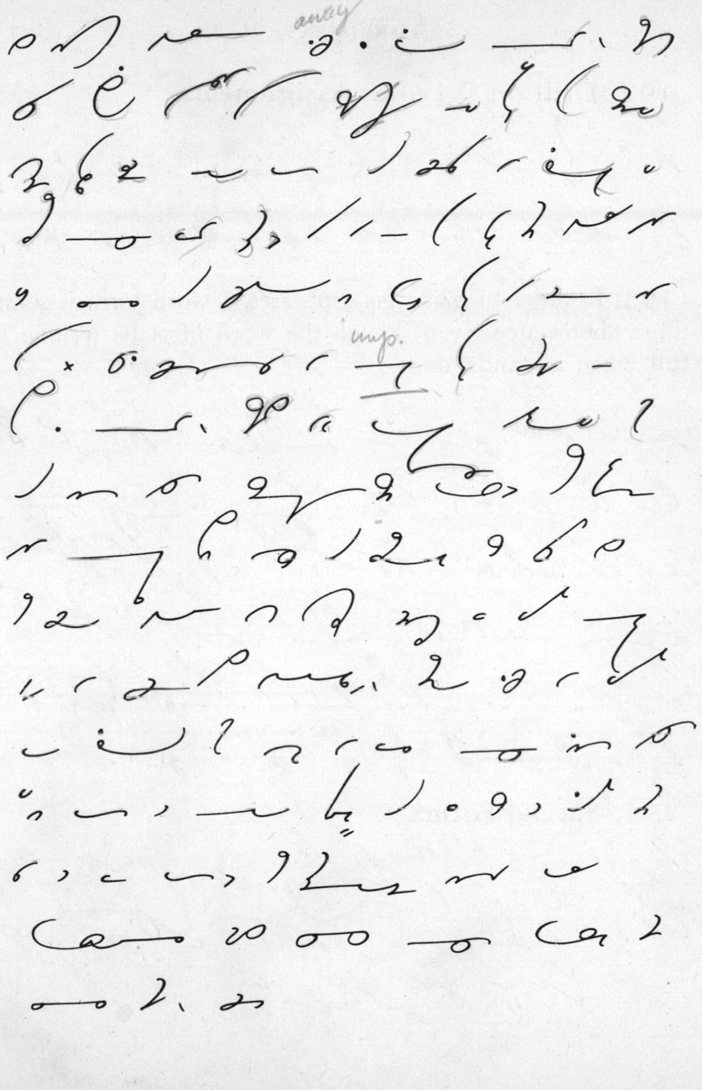

ASSIGNMENT 39

192. Drill on Previous Assignments

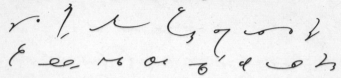

193. In order to make good phrases, a word form is sometimes abbreviated, even though the word must be written in full when it stands alone.

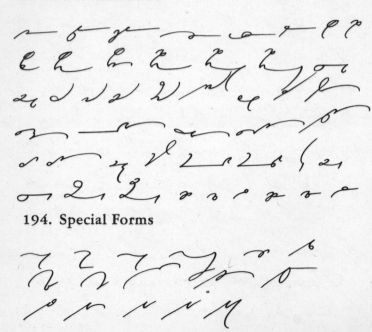

194. Special Forms

195. Reading and Writing Exercise

The Uncovered Blackboard

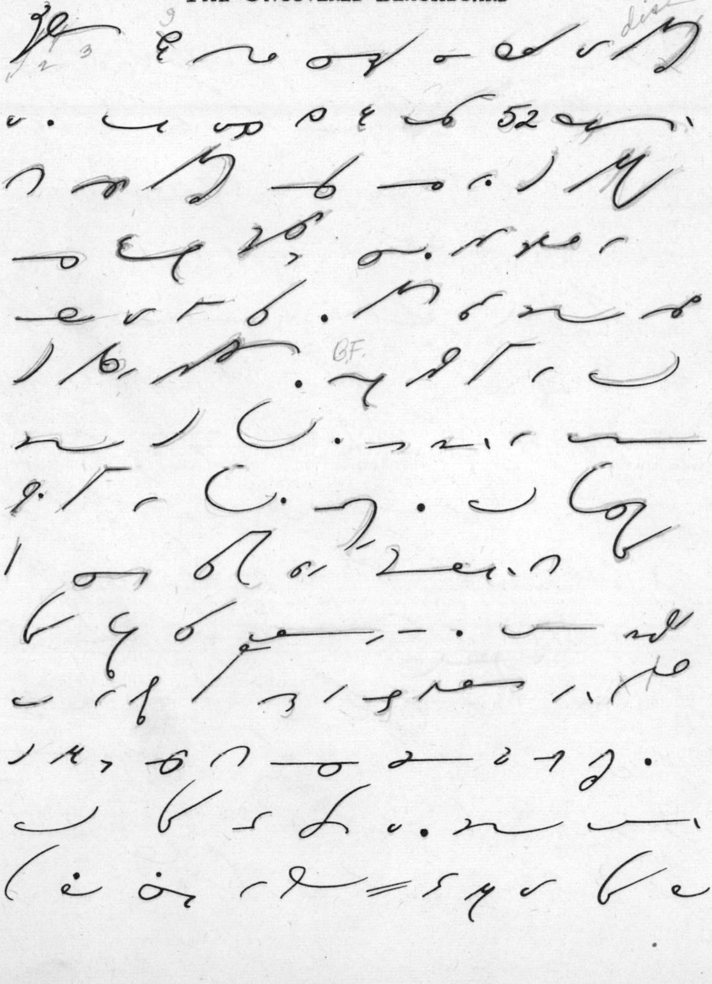

[Shorthand outlines spanning the page, including the dates "1881-1882"]

cultivated

Transcript of Shorthand

(Counted in groups of 20 standard words)

CHAPTER I

ASSIGNMENT 1

3. Ray, air, hair, rare, lay, ail, hail, rail.
4. Ray, rain, lay, lain, ail, nail.
5. Ache, make, cake, rake, lake, cane, came, gain, game.
6. *(a)* Ail, hail, rail, nail, tail, dale, gale. *(b)* Eel, heel, kneel, meal. *(c)* Ray, rain, train, drain, rate, read. *(d)* Lay, lain, lean, clean, lame, claim, late, lead, laid, lady. *(e)* Cane, game, aim, make, may, main, made, aid, day, tea, deed. *(f)* Meet, me, knee, mean, heat.

ASSIGNMENT 2

7. *(a)* Hat, adding, ham, cat, cattle, mat, mad, man. *(b)* Hack, tack, rack, lacking.
8. Dark, marking, lark, calm.
9. Hit, drilling, limit, kick, middle, trick.
10. Getting, ticket, merry, linen, headache, metal, wreck.
11. Can, go-good, are-our-hour, will-well, it-at, would, in-not, am-more, a-an, the, their-there, I, he.

✓ **12.** I can, I cannot, he can, he cannot, I can go, he can go, I will, he will, he will not, I am, it will, there will, in the, in it, they are, they will.

13. Thin, thick, theme, teeth, thrilling, thread.

15. Reading Exercise

Ray had a meal late in the day. Will Mary eat a meal in the train? Mary would take tea. Ray will claim Mary will[1] not eat a meal in the train. Her headache will delay her. A man will heat the tea. He will not heat the meat in the[2] metal kettle.

I will not read the theme in the dark. I would read the theme in a day. A man can go mad reading[3] a theme in the dark. I will make Mary take clean linen. Larry will make merry in the dale. He will greet me[4] in an hour.

I am not well. I will not go in the rain. A day in the good air will aid me. I will make the lame[5] lad eat a meal in the good air. He will get good milk there. I will take an egg a day. The milk will make the lad well.[6] He can make merry at the lake.

The greedy man ate the cake in the crate late in the day. The cake had lain in the[7] dark mill a day. The man cannot eat the ham. The cat ate the ham. It made the thin man mad.

I cannot hear him well,[8] can he hear me? The team will hear the tale I will read. The team will get cream in the train. Our team will gain a thrilling[9] game.

The hat lay there an hour. The lady will take the hat. Our maid will clean it. The maid will not aid the lad in kicking[10] the hat. The maid will hit the lad.

Ann made the cattle go in the train. Her gay air will not aid her in making[11] the cattle go in the train. The cattle will eat the grain in the train. The man made the grain at the mill. Will Ann hurry?[12] The mayor will not lag. He will need the deed Ann had at the mill The mayor will get the deed in an hour.

Amy[13] hid her hat in the tree. The lad at the gate will take the hat. Ann will not dream the lad will take the hat. Ann met[14] the lad at the tree. The lad will meet Ann at the hill in a day. Ann will get her hat.

I cannot get the ticket.[15] I cannot go. I am ill. I hear Eddy will aid me in Erie in May. He cannot get there in an hour in[16] the gray hack. The train came in late. A wreck made the main train late.

Ella will heat tea at the lake. The tea may aid Mary[17] in getting well. Her Dad will aid Mary in getting well, will he not? The thick cream I am getting will go in[18] the tea. The air at the lake will make Mary get well. Mary lay there an hour at the lake.

Ray had a lame leg. An[19] enemy hit him in the knee. He will hit the gay lark in the tree. A good aim will aid him, will it not? The lark[20] had an egg in the tree.

Mary had red hair. Her red hair will not make her mean, will it? I claim it will not. Her red[21] hair cannot make her mean. The green thread in her red hat may make her mean. Mary will greet Ray. He will eat the cake Mary[22] made. He cannot eat it at the lake, can he? He can eat the cake Mary made at the lake.

The man at the game[23] will take the ticket at the gate. I need a nickel. I cannot get in the arena. The man at the gate will[24] attack me.

I read the data at the meeting. I will not read the data at the league meeting. I cannot get[25] the main data. (502 standard words)

ASSIGNMENT 3

16. Add, added, heed, heeded, need, needed, treat, treated, hate, hated, rate, rated, detail.

17. Many-money, meant, mend, mental, month, minute, memory, eliminate.

18. The, they, that, great, with, without, Mr.-market, than then, them, of, be-by-but, is-his, this, to-too-two, and-end, you your, was, Yours truly, Dear Sir-desire.

19. Reading Exercise

Our team will meet the Erie men in a month. This Erie team is a great team. Our team is a great team, too, and cannot[1] be eliminated. The men hated to go to Erie. The rate by rail to Erie was more than Mr.[2] Lee had with him. Mr. Lee is the head man of the team, but his money is limited. The team would not be in[3] the league without Mr. Lee. The men would aid Mr. Lee in a minute. He is good to them. Many of the men[4] needed clean linen, and Mr. Lee had his maid get it. They needed it, but they would not take it. Then he made them[5] take it. They hated taking it, but in the end they did take it.

The train was late, but the track that will lead to Maine[6] was mended today and the train will be at the market in a minute. The memory of the man at the head[7] of the train is not good, but that will not mean the train will be late.

Many of the men in the train added that the[8] track would make a wreck that would thrill the lad kneeling in the dale. Would you be calm with a great wreck at the lake?

I desire[9] to go to the arena. Will you take me there? Is there a ticket that I can take? Mr. Lee is by the[10] gate and I cannot get in the arena without a ticket. I added the money that was in the clean metal[11] can, but I need more money than is there. I could not make a rainy day merry with the money that is in[12] that metal can. Can I get aid in the dairy? I would be ready to go to the market to get thread, but I[13] cannot remain to clean the dairy.

The maid came in with a good meal. There was thick cream in the tea, too. The lame lad[14] was treated to this good tea. His main desire was to eat more of the good meat Mary had made with the aid of Mr.[15] Drake. The lad cannot go to the lake without aid. His leg was hit by the limited train. He was hurrying[16] to get to the tree at the lake and then the train hit his leg. Mary was by the tree at the lake. (337 standard words)

Dear Sir: Is a day in May too late to get the data to you? I would not delay more than a day, but the data[1] are not ready. The lad that is to take the data to you is not here today. He hurried to the train with[2] the data, but could not make the train. Yours truly, (48 standard words)

Dear Sir: There was an error in the rate to Erie. I am going by train to Erie, but I would not dream of[1] meeting that rate. I am going to the great retail market there in Erie, and I cannot be late. I cannot[2] take a minute today to eliminate the error. Yours truly, (52 standard words)

Dear Sir: The hat may not be ready in a month. I desire to get that green hat. Will you clean it? There was a metal[1] tag in that hat. That meant that the hat would not be ready in a day. There will be a green hat at the market[2] today, but you cannot get it without money. The hat Mr. Lee had at the mill is a good hat. The hat is[3] gray, but there is a red thread in the middle. He will eliminate the red thread. The hat without the thread is neat.[4] I will take a dark hat to the game. This dark hat will be clean at the end of the day. There will not be a mark there.[5] Yours truly, (102 standard words)

ASSIGNMENT 4

20. Great, without, them, in this, be-by-but, was, and-end, Mr.-market, I can, there will, he will, Yours truly, their-there, you would, Dear Sir-desire, at that, by the, than-then, in it, I will not.

21. Did-date, other, all, were, where-aware, my, when, any, could, what, truth, time, into, come, like, little, those, country.

22. To the, to this, to that, to those, to them, to you, in the, in this, in that, in those, in them, into the, into this, into that, into those, into them, by those, with those, of those, it was, what was, where was, when was, and was, and I am, and I will, and I will be, I could, I could not, I could be, would not, did not, he could be, you could, I come, I came, you come, you came.

23. Reading Exercise

A COUNTRY INN

Would you like to go to the country where the air is good?

Come to Green Inn and you will hate to go when your time is[1] at an end. What time would you like to come to the country?

Green Inn is a little red and gray country inn in a[2] glen by Green Lake. There is a trail by the little creek at the rear of the inn. It will take you by an elm tree to[3] the granary and the dairy. This is an inn that was needed here and it was well that Henry and Harry had[4] money to get this acre. It was a good deed to get an inn here by the lake. Their aim is to get money by[5] making other men gay and merry.

Mr. and Mrs. Drake are here all the time. Their creed is to treat all men alike.[6] They clean all linen. They will get you clean linen and it will not be ragged, but it will[7] be well mended. The lady will mend your linen, too, when it is ragged and in need of mending.

You could come here[8] and remain a month and it would not take all your time to get here. Did you remain a month at the other inn that[9] is in Erie? Take a train at Lynn and it will get you here to the inn. Mr. Drake will meet you at the train with[10] a team and a rig and he will take you to Green Lake. You can then take the lane at the end of the lake and that will[11] lead you to the gate of Green Inn. It will be late when you get here, but Mrs. Drake will be here to greet you, and a[12] good meal with ham and turkey will be ready at that time.

Your money may be limited but that will not mean that[13] you cannot come here. All you need is a little money. You will gain when you are here. The lake air is good and it[14] will make you eat well. You will get clean milk, thick cream, and good cake. There will not be any liquor at this inn. There will[15] be little racket here. You will get rid of a headache and any other ache you may be eager to eliminate.[16]

All men that come here can be gay and merry. You can go into the lake when it is calm. You can go when[17] there will not be a gale. You may add to your technique in any game you desire. Ned Taylor is here all the time[18] and he is a man with good technique in handling a racquet and a net and in hitting a mark. He can train the[19] eye, the hand, and the ear in any game. You can get a caddy by the hour at a minimum rate, and you can[20] drill hour by hour in making a gain in your technique.

The attic of the inn is heated when heat is needed. The attic is not dark. It is a clean attic and Mrs. Drake is neat in handling it. Her canary is there to[21] add to the merry air of it. Her cat is in the granary where it cannot get to the canary but where[22] it can get a rat.

This inn is well rated by many leading men. The mayor, Mr. Allen, and Dr. Ray[23] were here a month. Mrs. Drake treated them well and they would like to come at a late date in May. You would get the truth[24] in their keen rating of it. (485 standard words)

CHAPTER II

ASSIGNMENT 5

24. Like, could, without, great, was, my, did-date, other, will be, he will not, I would, they are, they will, I could not, in this, of those.

25. Put, pay, paper, camp, map, pair, trip, happen, pretty. Be-by-but, bay, bare, bail, brain, blame, back, beat, bury.

26. For, fare, affair, fame, fear, feel, if, factory, free. Have, heavy, leave, relieve, victory, even, valley.

27. Shall-ship, cash, shade, dash, shame, mash, sharp, finish, shell. Change-which, check, catch, chain, match, cheap, peach, chief, fetch. Age, edge, jail, jelly, page, range, ledge, bridge.

28. One, after, people, about, most, form-from, been-bound, very, before, much, never, should, over, ever, every, Dear Madam, Very truly yours, Yours very truly.

29. Reading Exercise

Getting Ready for the Fair

There is about a month left before fair time in the valley and every lady in the country is getting ready[1] for it. Each will put in much time and labor before it is over.

Mr. and Mrs. Lee live at the ranch.[2] They plan to take much to the fair this time and much of it is ready. Their fame for making money at the fair is[3] gaining, but they have never won over their neighbor. They should get much money for their labor this time and they will[4] if they ever get a victory over this neighbor.

Even with a maid to help her, Mrs. Lee is putting[5] in an hour and more over her magic range in her kitchen every day. Her jam is rich and red. Today she is[6] canning chicken which will be taken to the fair too. After the canning is over for the day, a label is[7] put with each can before it is put in a bag.

Sitting in her parlor she was making a cap for a baby,[8] a lamp shade, and a bag. She will finish a linen sheet which she is making. She will make a tag and pin one to[9] each and then pack them in a bag. Before she and Mr. Lee leave for the trip to the fair, she will put this bag in[10] the back of the machine in the garage.

The day before they go, she and her maid should be in the kitchen at daybreak,[11] finishing what she will take to the fair before it is too late in the day. Bread will be baked and cake will be[12] made. They cannot ever be made more than a day before the fair, for they should be very fresh. She will pick a pretty[13] peach and put it in a green dish with a red apple and a pear and they are bound to take one ribbon.

Mr.[14] Lee is getting ready for the fair too. He is feeding a fat pig. He will take his calf and the turkey with him.[15] He may take his sheep and a little lamb too, but he will settle that before the day of the fair. (317 standard words)

Dear Sir: I should like to get a plan for a little shed made by you. I feel I should have one before it is too[1] late in the month. If you could make the frame for me, I can finish it by the time it is needed. I will put paper[2] over the frame and then put the brick over the paper. I feel that that would make a good shed for the sheep.

If[3] you can come by the middle of this month, may I hear from you? I shall be ready to help you. Very truly yours,[4] (80 standard words)

Dear Sir: Our plan is to get a brick cabin in the valley leading to the bay where people can go for a picnic[1] and play at the beach. The trip to the bay by ship is a cheap and rapid one. People can leave here before daybreak[2] and remain late, having the day in the country by the lake. After a day at the beach in the fresh air, most[3] people are bound to get a happy feeling.

Read the clipping from our evening paper about the federal money[4] that will aid in paying for the brick, if our branch can get the cash for the labor before May 1.

I shall need[5] very much help to get the needed cash by that date and I should like your help. I shall have my plan for this campaign[6] in good form by the end of this month. If you can come here about that time, I shall check every detail of that plan[7] with you. Yours very truly, (145 standard words)

ASSIGNMENT 6

30. Paper, happen, trip, bear, bail, free, frame, even, finish, check, catch, age, page, before, much, should, about, people, one, Dear Madam.

31. Had been, have been, I have been, you have been, have not been, I have not been, you have not been, has been, it has been, there has been, what has been.

32. From the, from this, from that, from those, from them, from which, from which the, about the, about this, about that, about those, about them, about which, before the, before this, before that, before those, before them, by which, in which, of which, and which, very much, very good, very well, should be, I should be, he should be, I should not, I should have, I should have been, you would have been, I would have been, he would have been.

33. To be, to have, to pay, to fill, to plan, to blame, to form.

34. Reading Exercise

Dear Madam: Our people are in the habit of helping with

the welfare of a neighbor in need, and they have been[1] very good when there is ever a welfare campaign to put over. But it is a shame that they have never[2] had any plan to help those living in the factory region. I am making my chief appeal this month in their behalf to each member of the League.

You may not be aware that many laboring people have had very little[3] change from month to month. They labor much of the time but there is time left for them to play after they finish their labor[4] every day. The pity is that when they happen to have a free day most of them can never take a penny[5] from their pay for a trip to the beach to vary their living. What they make at the factory is needed for bread and[6] other plain living.

My plan is to put a cabin in the park by the beach where people can go for a day without[7] any need of money. The League should pay their fare over and back for them and they could be fed at the cabin.[8] A maid should be there each day to play with a baby—that would leave the people free to play at the beach and to fish.[9]

Would you like to help in this welfare plan? Can you help with your money today? Would you make a pledge for a check each[10] month? I shall be happy to hear from you about this plan and your desire about paying if you can help. Very[11] truly yours, (222 standard words)

Dear Sir: A cheap letter paper coming from his desk never won a campaign for any man.

For your campaign I[1] should like to get for you a heavy sheet of paper with a plain black heading. My bid for it would not be more than[2] you have been paying for paper and the gain would be an immense one. After your campaign for mayor is won—you[3] are bound to beat Mr. Edge in his battle with you—I could add a bit to the heading and make it most fitting[4] to come from the desk of the mayor.

Would you like to hear more about my plan? Very truly yours, (92 standard words)

Dear Madam: I have not had to pack any of my cream for you in many a day. Maybe you are not aware[1] of one flavor which I have added and am making most every day. You will like this fresh peach cream and come back for[2] more if you ever have any of it. It is rich and creamy. Would you not like to have one brick of vanilla[3] cream for a change?

If you are bound for a picnic, I shall be happy to pack each brick of cream in a bag that will[4] eliminate any fear of melting before you are ready for it. I can take it over for you any[5] hour before you go. Very truly yours, (107 standard words)

Dear Sir: I have a crane which came from your factory. I did not get much heavy lifting from it before there was[1] a break in it. You led me to feel that this should not happen.

I cannot be without the crane for the time it would[2] take to ship it to you and get it back from you. I left it in a garage here for mending and it was put back[3] in good form by the man there.

I shall get the ticket which came from the garage man. Would you be willing to pay this[4] fee for his labor? Yours very truly, (87 standard words)

Dear Sir: I cannot blame you for the feeling you have about the shape in which your chapel was left after our meeting[1] the other evening. When the man was able to get it for his meeting without paying for it in any[2] form, he should have left it clean and neat. There was never any need of leaving it as he did.

I shall have my men[3] come to help you clean it today.
Yours truly, (67 standard words)

35. Changing, shall-ship, Yours very truly, every, for, about, most, little, those, into, did-date, country, there will, I could not, I did not, what has been, there has been, has been, it has been, to be, to have, to put, had been, I was.

36. Spare, spread, helps, lamps, maps, space, busy, bears, dress, neighbors, papers, trace, selling, salary, sales, apples, feels, meals, place, palace, gifts, hats, minutes, months, plates, tickets, brains, chance, dance, happens, trance, games, task, least.

37. Say, see, seen, seem, same, set, said, easy, case, makes, sake, scheme, takes, skate, eggs, guess, stage, stay, stayed, steam, straight, face, safe, safety, cease, season, these, reaches, teaches, branches, ages, pages, dashes, visit, guest.

38. Reading Exercise

SHIPPING GOODS

Busy men at one factory pack their goods in barrels and nail stiff lids over the heads of the barrels. Men at[1] other factories put their goods in sacks, in baskets, and in chests. The goods can be packed in any form,[2] if they take as little space as is needed for a safe trip. They should seal them before releasing them for shipping[3] to the other city for sale by retail branches.

When they are ready, the barrel is taken to the scales to[4] see if it is heavy. After a glance at the tariff sheets, the man at the desk marks the label and the sheets with[5] the fee. He stamps each one with the date. One sheet will go with the sales slip to the retail branch to be checked when the goods[6] get there. They may be left by the tracks to be taken by trains from the platform to the people desiring them.

The[7] chance of reaching the branch in time and in good shape is more than a fair one and there seems to be very little risk.[8] But even with a steel train there is a chance of a crash that will smash the goods. There is a chance, too, that the goods will[9] go astray and that they will be many days late in reaching the end of their trip—too late to be of much good to[10] the retail man. They may even perish before they get there. In one season apples and goods of that class freeze, and[11] in other seasons they perish from heat.

The one shipping the goods will fill in forms and place a claim for the goods. If[12] the goods go astray, a tracer goes after them. If the goods are of a class that perishes with ease, a sale of[13] them may take place before they perish and the money from this sale will help in settling the claim. Errors are bound to[14] happen but they should not happen every day. (287 standard words)

Dear Sir: I should like you to ship your goods in the bags which I have for sale. These bags are easier to handle than[1] wrapping paper in shipping the class of goods you sell. They vary in shape and in the space left for the goods.

Wrapping[2] goods in these bags makes for safety, too, and leads to a saving in claims to settle, since goods stay in the bags after[3] sealing.

All your shipping help will like them since they are easy to handle. You will like them, too, for the immense saving[4] in

time, labor, and cash. When would you like to see them?
Yours truly, (92 standard words)

Dear Sir: At a meeting of the sales staff, I should like you
to say much about the desk which I have to sell. Its brass[1]
handles and little panes of glass make it a pretty desk.

It fits in a little space but it has much space in it[2] and fills
many needs. It could take the place of a chest for linens.
It has shelves for papers of all shapes. Yours very[3] truly,
(61 standard words)

Dear Sir: This is the season when one begins to need
screens.

Screens are of steel mesh, with plain metal frames. They
are not cheap[1] but they are a good fit. They are less apt to
change shape after seasons of rain and heat. Even at that,
they should not[2] be left in place when not needed after a
freezing day. They are easy to put back as they have hinges
at one[3] end.

Visit Mr. Lee's factory in your city and after seeing it, listen
to what he has to say[4] about the screens. If you are then in
the market for them, I shall have a man come and bid on
them for your factory.[5] Yours very truly, (103 standard
words)

Assignment 8

39. After, put, did-date, people, my, all, most, for, shall-
ship, could, form-from, come, time, Dear Sir-desire, Mr.-
market, what, great, am-more, much, them, truth, other, this,
without, when, any, where-aware, every, is-his, change-which,
little, should, be-by-but, like, than-then, over, and-end, to-too-
two, from them, I should be, into that, has been, and I will
be, with those.

40. Sense, senses; case, cases; face, faces; chance, chances; dance, dances; place, places; dress, dresses; trace, traces.

41. Under, must, some, such, first, business, cause-because, thorough-thoroughly-three, thing-think, system-says, far-favor, public-publish, work, part, matter, again, against, always, anything, something, everything.

42. Hours, yours, dates, others, truths, times, countries, changes, ships, forms, businesses, causes, things, systems, publishes, works, parts, matters.

43. Reading Exercise

A Fairy Tale

There is a fairy tale about a man with one maid marrying a lady with two maids. The two were far from pretty[1] but had dresses of velvet and silk with rich laces and had many chances to go to parties. The other[2] maid was never in the lady's favor and because of that she never had a silk dress and pretty slippers to[3] go with it. For this cause, too, she was always busy cleaning plates in the kitchen and working at tasks for the two[4] other maids. She was pretty, but even in her ragged dresses she was much prettier than the others.[5]

One evening when the other maids were having a good time at the prince's dance, which he was in the habit of having[6] at his palace, she finished the dishes and then sat dreaming and thinking. After the lapse of a little time,[7] a fairy came to visit her. The fairy had made an analysis of what was causing her to be sad, and[8] had a secret scheme to get some chances for the little lady to take part in the dances.

First the fairy had[9] the maid get everything she needed, and then she cast a spell and made immense changes in each thing by passing her[10] stick over it. After this, there was never a trace of the rags left. In their place there was a dress of velvet and other goods with[11] sleeves of lace and slippers of glass. There were little pages to help her with her train and some prancing steeds because she[12] was to be driven to the dances which the prince was having at his palace far from the city. At least, she was[13] going places this evening!

But before she left, the fairy said that she must[14] leave the dance at a set hour, if she were to get back in safety. That evening, against her desires because she was[15] having a thoroughly good time, she left the party at the set hour and was back before the other maids came. As[16] she sat listening to their tales of the fascinating lady that had won the favor of the prince, she was thinking[17] of her part but she never said a thing about her having been that lady.

Again this same fairy came and[18] made the series of changes which meant a chance for the sad one to go as a guest to the dances, but that evening[19] her happiness made the minutes pass in such a hurry that she never had any memory of what the fairy[20] had said about leaving. When the first peal of the bell that says the time of day reached her ears, she left the dance in[21] great haste. In her haste to get to her chamber before the bell ceased, one of her slippers fell and was left at the dance.[22] But she stayed some minutes too late and before she reached her chamber not a scrap of the rich dress was left. She was in[23] rags, and she did not have anything left but the other glass slipper which had not been left at the dance.

The prince had[24] met her the first evening and had some

dances with her each time she was there. Because she was his favorite guest, he[25] missed her after she left. With the glass slipper as a basis, he set about to trace her by having a thorough[26] canvass of the city made. The prince made it his business to have some of his men publish his plan to marry the one that the[27] slipper would fit.

When one man came to their part of the city, the two maids had chances to have the glass slipper fit,[28] but in vain. When the lady in rags said she would like a chance, they laughed at her. Against their desires, the man fitted[29] the slipper. The slipper was a good fit for her, and under her lashes she cast a glance at their faces when she[30] put before them the one to match it. That was a help in settling the matter and her part in it.

By some mystery,[31] the fairy came at that very minute and with fast passes of her stick she again made changes in the dress[32] of the maid before their very faces.

The fairy tale ends with the man taking the pretty lady to the palace[33] where the prince married her. You may have three guesses as to which lady this tale has been published about. (678 standard words)

ASSIGNMENT 9

44. Again, matters, some, under, far-favor, working, everything, public-publish, always, anything, against, systems, cause-because, must, thorough-thoroughly-three, business, first, such, much, put, shall-ship, have, for, it has been, I have not been, before the, very good, I should be, from them, it was.

45. Miss, mix; misses, mixes; fix, fixes; tax, taxes.

46. Nation, action, mention, fashion, section, election, vacation, relation.

47. Caused, changed, desired, favored, formed, liked, parted, shipped.

48. Saved, traced, checked, fixed, marked, placed.

49. Also, nothing, between, another, woman, morning, letter-let, present-presence, big-beg, give-given, till-tell, tells, still, until, got, gave, next, soon, name.

50. Reading Exercise

Taxes

The raising of money with which to pay debts and finance the public business is always an immense task for the[1] members of the Senate and the members of the other national chamber. The tax system of the country is[2] always changing because each time there is an election there are changes in the members of these chambers.

These men[3] have given much time to the study and analysis of the tax system because during their campaigns for[4] election they have said much about the present taxes and have mentioned what should be changed. When these men begin their work,[5] changes in the tax plans will be made; hence the people should listen when these men say anything about taxes.

People[6] pay taxes in this country. The nation taxes any money that people may make. The rate is fixed by the[7] men in the Senate and the other chamber. The money a man makes is a fair basis for taxes. Men with much[8] money can pay more than those having a little salary.

All men pay some taxes. The rich man and the laboring[9] man are treated the same. Each plays his part in giving money for the welfare of the nation.

There is another[10] thing in favor of taxing what a man makes. The tax cannot be shifted to other people. The men making[11] the money must pay the tax. This tax is not like other taxes, because it cannot be shifted. The more money[12] a man makes, the bigger the tax he will have to pay. Laboring men that dig ditches need not pay this tax because[13] they get less than the minimum that is taxed.

There is also a tax when gifts are given and when money is left[14] to the heirs of very rich people. These taxes raise much money from people that can pay and will not miss what they[15] pay.

The tariff is another Federal tax. This tax is for goods shipped into this country. The rates vary because[16] it is desired to give people in this country a chance to sell goods that may be made for less in other countries.[17] This tax is shifted to others. The man paying the tax adds it to what you pay for his goods.

When people come[18] back here from trips to neighboring countries and countries over the sea, they have dresses, hats, and presents with them. They[19] must pay a duty if they have more than the maximum. Many have evaded paying this tax.

Some goods are taxed[20] in this country, too. The people making these goods pay the tax by paying cash and getting a stamp for it. They must[21] stick a stamp over the wrapping of each piece of goods they sell. This tax is another that can be shifted from the[22] maker of the goods to the people that get them.

There are also many other taxes in the Federal system[23] that have been added when more money was needed because of some great undertaking. A tax for tickets gets[24] much money from people that can pay it without feeling it too much. This tax adds to what they pay for having a[25] good time. Still, they should not have to pay such a big tax.

A gasoline tax soon seems very heavy to the man with[26] a machine. He feels that he is paying more than he should.

Our country has reached a stage where some other taxes may[27] be needed to help pay back all the money the nation is giving for the relief of those that have not had work[28] for many months. The next tax plan may be passed very soon. Other taxes may be added to those the people are[29] paying today. Many business men favor a retail sales tax to be levied against goods that the business men[30] sell. This could be shifted by them to the people getting the goods.

Everything which has been said about taxes here[31] may be changed by the time you are ready to help in the selection of the men making our taxes. You must study[32] about them all the time by reading the books and the papers telling of the changes that are being made from[33] month to month. Then you can place a mark against the name of the man that is in favor of the tax plan that appeals[34] to you. (681 standard words)

ASSIGNMENT 10

51. Name, favored, also, thorough-thoroughly-three, between, shipping, morning, for, letter-let, systems, another, changed, big-beg, something, until, come, got, little, presents, my, when, woman, have, nothing, did-date, still, great, soon,

I could not, I would not, he would be, into the, to this, has been, Dear Madam.

52. Almost, income, increase, ago, inform, underneath, handle, forgive, begin.

53. For the, for this, for that, for those, for these, for them, for you, there is, there was, there are, there will be, if you would, if you would be, if you are, if you are not, if you will, if you will be, I have given, I have never, I have not been.

54. Reading Exercise

A LITTLE PIN

"I would not steal a little pin" is a saying that has little meaning for the people of the present day, as[1] any woman would give you a pin if you desired it. Almost anyone would give you a pin.

I need not inform[2] you that pins fill many needs. They are easy to get, but we could not live without them. Pins range from big heavy[3] safety pins to the little steel pins that may be seen in a lady's dresser. Many is the hem that was fixed with the aid[4] of a pin. Pins are good helpers.

I should like to tell you the tale of a steel pin from the time it was placed[5] in a neat little paper at the factory until this day. This pin and the other pins in the same paper[6] had a merry time from the day they left the factory. This is the tale of one little pin as it was given[7] me:

"One day a lady came for me and the other pins in the same paper with me. She put me in a tray at her place of business.[8] I was taken from my pals in the paper. Here my labors began, pinning hems and helping[9] this woman make many changes in pretty dresses. When I finished my labors for the day, I was put back in[10] the tray until I was needed again. I liked this very much but, like every other good thing, this soon came to[11] an end. One day I was left sticking in the sleeve of a silk dress.

"Since the woman did not see me when she fitted[12] the dress, I, too, had to go to the dance. As she got her wrap and was going to leave the scene of the dance, I fell[13] from the dress and lay in a dark crack into which I slipped. After many days, a lad came by. Seeing me, he put[14] me into the edge of his jacket. Again I was about to live and work, but what varied tasks were given[15] me. I was made to stick into desks and into people as they sat at them; I was placed at the end of a big[16] stick with a piece of paper spinning in the air; I was put into places that I did not like.

"After a month[17] of this work I was getting eager to slip from this lad's grasp and go with other people to other sections of[18] the country and even to other nations.

"Everything comes in time, and my chance soon came. I fell from the grasp of[19] the lad into a dark alley where I feared I should never be seen again, as I was far from any public[20] place. But another woman, visiting with a neighbor over the fence, stepped in the path where I lay and, catching[21] a glimpse of me, raised me from the earth and placed me in her dresser. This dresser was like the one where I lived many[22] happy months when I first left my pals that came with me from the factory.

"This lady liked to go in airplanes. One[23] day her airplane fell to earth. She was saved by a man that would not give his name, but I remained in the plane.

"Then began[24] days of action, days of thrills and many

risks. I missed death at times by less than a hair's breadth.

"I needed a change.[25] I craved nothing more than release from my work for a little time. One morning I slipped under a heap of papers[26] that were being taken into the cellar. I have been in the cellar for some days. Soon I will be ready to[27] go back to the task of living again."

As the tale ended, I said: "The time has come, little pin, for you to go[28] back." I put the pin in the lapel of my jacket. The time will come when I shall give this little pin another[20] chance to get before the public again. (587 standard words)

CHAPTER III

ASSIGNMENT 11

55. Make, nail, jail, need, needle, ham, cattle, map, drill, trip, dark.

57. No, toe, low, blow, hope, ocean, notion, motion, narrow, obey, open, fellow, globe, drove, rode, rope, so, sore, soul, soap, show, shown, showed, grow, hero.

58. Raw, brought, broad, abroad, ball, caution, cross, draw, law, ought, saw, salt, talk, talked, taught, withdraw.

59. Hot, top, lot, shop, shot, solid, sorry, sorrow, job, lock, block, hospital, knock, spot.

60. Own, known, alone, tone, stone, home, omit, or, door, nor, orange, hall, coal, college.

61. Reading Exercise

Globe Trotting

Did you hear about the trip abroad that Joan and I made? I often talked with Joan about it but no plans were made.[1] I did not think of going at that time as I could not go without borrowing money. I could not go to college[2] because of my lack of money and going abroad was far from my thoughts, until Maud wrote that her folks were thinking[3] of going globe trotting and were eager to have me go with them. I did not think I should leave my job at the[4] shop, but it was nonsense to stay at home, so after sober thinking I obeyed my desire and posted a letter[5] telling her I would meet them at the hotel on the coast for the beginning of a jolly time in the countries[6] abroad.

My first job was to get some clothes. I needed much, but as my pocketbook showed that there was little money[7] with which to get everything I needed, I fought off the desire to get lots of fashion models and chose a[8] soft hat for the boat, a heavy topcoat and some hose.

I reached the city in the evening and the hotel auto[9] brought me to the door of the hotel. I crossed the great hall and there I met Maud. After I gave her my wraps, Maud sat[10] on the bench and she and I talked until some other people began to come to the lower hall to eat. Chops and potatoes[11] tasted pretty good and then a pot of good coffee was brought on. When the meal was over, my thoughts were on the trip.[12]

Crossing the ocean was fascinating during the whole time. There was a little gale one day which drove the people[13] from the decks of the boat but it was soon over and the motion of the boat began to be easy again. The[14] boat docked at Dover and the folks were taken in autos to the hotels. Here I saw the stores packed close to each other.[15] Then we came to the country roads with rows and rows of hedges.

I was sorry to leave, but the next day I was[16] on the boat again and off for France. I liked Paris and was sorry I could not stay and roam all alone in the[17] stores and get some trophies. As I could not talk French, though, I did not have an easy time of it. It was appalling[18] at first because I could not shop. I saw flocks of sheep and goats roaming over the open hills. There were acres and[19] acres of grapes.

After Paris and France came Rome and Venice, and I could talk for many hours about what I[20] saw there. In Venice the black boats floated on the narrow canals. I remained in Venice for a day and then was[21] off for Rome.

After Rome came Naples and after leaving Naples the boat was bound for home. It was a jolly[22] holiday, but I showed no sorrow when I saw the harbor and the lofty steeples of the city. I brought many[23] stories and glowing memories and loads of trophies from the shops to show to folks here. Much as I liked all the scenes[24] over the sea, still it was good to be at home. It was good to hear the roar of the trolleys and to see so many[25] autos pass by. Though it is a relief to go abroad for a month or two I would not live there all the time.[26] (520 standard words)

ASSIGNMENT 12

62. Low, blow, toe, notion, obey, known, loan, brought, abroad, ball, draw, salt, talk, top, spot, lot, block, solid, sorry.

63. Want, went, told, order, small, upon, glad-girl, doctor-during, believe-belief, possible, purpose, receive, call, situation, course, general, several, state.

64. Want, wanted, wants, wanting, order, orders, ordered, ordering, glad, gladden, gladness, believe, believes, believed, believing, receive, receives, received, receiving, call, calls, calling, called, recall, situation, situations, course, courses, state, states, stating, stated, estate.

65. I believe, I cannot believe, I receive, I received, he receives, he received, they receive, they received, I have received, upon the, upon that, upon this, upon these, upon those, upon them, I told, he told, told you, told me, I told you, he told me, I have told, several times, several days.

66. Reading Exercise

Hobbies

Everyone believes, in general, that games and hobbies are a needed change from any job, and are an aid to[1] the system. Work, so-called, is something that must be achieved during the course of a stated time. It is something that[2] one is called upon to undertake because he is ordered to. Often the same thing is brought about because one[3] wanted and chose to undertake it without orders, and so it is fascinating play. So, the little girl taught[4] to sew will, as a general matter, pause when shown a little hole that must be mended, but will sew for her doll[5] for several hours of a morning with gladness. Bringing coal from the cellar for the stove is a task for a lad[6] I know, but upon being told that it has snowed during his sleep, he, like a score that you may recall, will be[7] glad to haul snow all day for a snow man.

It is the same when playing games. It would be a bore to be ordered to[8] some spot and back again a score of times, but call it "a crow race," and the whole situation takes on another[9] tone. A fellow would go to the grocery without too many pauses and think he were a hero because he[10] went without groaning, but would be glad to cross the whole country in the hope of getting a lark with his bow and arrow.[11]

The grown lad plays on several ball teams. If called upon for that much time for work, he would think he should receive[12] money and would be very much fatigued at the end of a day, but he comes home from the ball game in a happy[13] state, recalling the applause he received in the course of the play. The busy business man, told by his doctor to[14] get more fresh air, would not think of leaving his auto at home more often and walking several blocks to his work.[15] No, he would order his auto, and be driven to the golf green. After receiving his sticks from his chauffeur and[16] placing them in the hands of a caddy, he would go upon the golf course, happy in the belief that this was[17] obeying the doctor's orders.

The role of hero is one that all are glad to be called upon to play, and the tall[18] college basket-ball player receives great applause, and this applause is something that is wanted by many people.[19]

When people are grown, they often call their play "hobbies." So some girls are glad that it is possible to stay at home[20] during the dark days of this season and they have dancing as their hobby. Others can see no possible purpose[21] in this. Some like the opera and could listen to the solos of the soprano several hours.

When the air[22] is soft and calls people from their homes, the general desire is for the country. Some feel that they must take their rod[23] and reel and fish from the shore of some lake. One man I know stated that he went on his holidays to a place where[24] he got arrow heads and he told me that it was his belief that this was a great hobby.

The camera is the[25] hobby of many people. Everyone owns at least a box camera which he can put in his coat pocket and[26] place on a fence when a trophy is sought. A person with this hobby, in general, will attack the enemy[27] almost without notice, on the lawn at home, in the meadows, or in the grove. Everyone is his game and it is[28] folly to dodge him as he pokes his camera at the enemy and closes in upon him.

It is all the[29] same, no matter what the situation, with the doctor or baker, girl or woman, lad or man, all must have some[30] portion of play mixed with their work to help their souls to be glad and to cause them to laugh and to overcome the ordered[31] tasks of the day. (623 standard words)

Assignment 13

67. Day, may, main, tea, deed, knee, me, mean, heat, heed, heeded, hate, hated, him, aim, went, order, small, doctor-during, possible, receive, several, state, situation, I receive, upon them, several times, he told me, told you, upon that, wanting, believed, calling, gladness, purposes, courses.

68. Dare, dear, near, mere, manner, sheer, cheer, share, chair, flatter, owner, former, sooner, leader, reader, richer, ledger, sister, steamer, visitor, register, art, heart, hard, hurt, heard, arm, harm, harmony, earn, urge, dirty, start, started, church, murmur.

69. Reading Exercise

THE HONOR OF THE TEAM

Bob sat in his chair and gazed on the green where the baseball team was getting ready to play. He was the leader of[1] the team and their honor was at stake, for the big team from Dearing was coming to play the next day and the game would[2] be a hard one. Bob was far from cheered when he saw them, for at the mere thought that he could not be with the[3] team and help tear a victory from the Dearing lads, he glanced at the chapter as he wrote, and so finished the lesson.[4] As he did it, he saw his sister staring at him, but she said nothing. During the major part of the[5] day he felt that the teacher and his sister were noticing his manner. But he earned his place on the team by hard[6] work.

The day of the game came and there was nothing to mar it but Bob's own feeling. It will be a hard and bitter[7] battle, and all the girls and fellows will be there with the class banner, the cheer leader, and all will be chattering[8] and cheering to stir the fellows to better playing. As Bob was on the stair near the door, he heard a teacher say[9] that he was a good leader because he worked harder at his studies than at his play. This hurt Bob and he started to[10] say, "No I am a cheater," but he thought that the team needed him and if he should tell, he would be put off the team.[11] But the day was marred for him. His sister had always praised him for being a good soldier and daring to be brave.[12] Well, after all, he could not take a place that he did not earn. Archie could play a good game in his place. He would tell[13] the teacher and not mar the honor of the team.

The time for the game came, and Archie was in his place and it was[14] hard to cheer even as he saw the scores being registered for his team. But what had taken place? A man was hurt.[15] The pitcher had thrown the ball and the batter had hit it far off to the left. Archie was nearer the ball and caught[16] it, but his arm was hurt and he was taken from the game, in a battered state. Bob dared not hope that he would be called,[17] but after a little talk, he heard his name and a cheer rose from the bleacher seats, as he ran to his place. Every batter shared in[18] the flattering applause. At the end of the game the honor went to Archie and Bob for making[19] the scores and it was with a glad heart that he could feel that everyone liked him better for not letting the mere desire for[20] playing get the better of his former habits of telling the truth and not being a cheater in work or play.[21] (420 standard words)

Dear Sir: The auditor has checked over our ledger, and our sales for these three months are near the mark set by you at[1] the start of our business here. Every debtor is honoring his notes and paying on time a good share of what he[2] owes. Our cash register shows good sales every day and our cashier says they are increasing since Easter. One factor[3] is the putting in of the paved road near our store, where the major part of the motor traffic must come. In the latter[4] part of this month I am going to start a campaign of sales to cater to the better class of people, and[5] in this manner hope to raise the tone of our store. Yours truly, (110 standard words)

Dear Reader: Our editor would like to give the reader a better paper, and the oftener you say what you[1] like, the more flattered he will be and the better paper you will have. In a sense, you are a partner and part owner[2] of our publication.

Is our manner of placing ads any neater or better? Is there too great a share[3] of fiction, and should the art work be a major factor? Would you like another chapter of the story, or would[4] it be better to adhere to the present plan of giving one chapter in each issue? You are urged to give any[5] help you can in any matter from grammar to finance. Nothing will be sneered at, for the editor will feel[6] that he is your debtor for any help you may give. If you will start sending in any notes you may have, they will[7] receive a hearty welcome. Yours truly, (147 standard words)

ASSIGNMENT 14

70. Day, dare, dear, tea, tear, knee, near, me, mere, many, manner, ready, reader, she, sheer, hate, heart, add, hard, aim, arm, harm, hit, hurt, inn, earn, edge, urge, head, heard, if you will, I have given, for them, there are, there will be, I cannot believe, orders, believing, recall, estate, between, woman, name, did-date, others.

71. Dares, manners, cheers, chairs, flatters, owners, leaders, readers, sisters, steamers, visitors, registers, ledgers.

72. Either, above, rather, love, collect, capital, deal-dear, real-regard, company-keep, book-become, importance-important, necessary, yesterday, together, children, prepare, subject, opinion.

7.3. Reading Exercise

A HARD TIMES STORY

Are hard times necessary to give this country greater and

better men, or, rather, is it that some folks have risen[1] above their lot and have become great, regardless of their situation?

When one sees great teachers, preachers, doctors,[2] editors, and soldiers, it is hard to think they have ever been dirty little lads, playing in a manner[3] that is the same as others; or sisters, sharing each others' dolls and dishes, and tearing their dresses as they scattered[4] in a game of tag. But all these great ones were the children of yesterday, near and dear to their folks.

When Dickens[5] was a little lad he would go and stare at a rich home on a hill and think that he would work hard and become the[6] owner of it. He liked to share the company of his sister, and they often went together in the evening[7] and gazed at the stars. He lived at one time in a debtors' prison because he did not have any capital and[8] you cannot think of a sadder preparation for later living than a place like this. Often he saw cakes in[9] the stores and shed bitter tears because he did not have anything to eat. Later, when times had become better and[10] he left the prison, he was a great favorite with other children because he could keep them happy with the stories[11] he told. He wrote stories telling about the debtors' prisons and many other important subjects dear to[12] his heart. He loved children and was sorry for those with little cheer in their homes, as he recollected his own hard[13] lot when he was small.

There was a little girl living in a garret in a dirty city. Her one playmate was[14] a doll with red cheeks, that kept staring regardless of good manners. She, too, had rather hard times and little company[15] of other children until she went to the country. Here she studied hard, loved and read many books, and had more[16] company than in the city. One day she met a lady that urged her to dance in a play together with other[17] children. Either because it was necessary for her to get capital, or because this was a great chance[18] in her opinion to be with other children, she did it, and it was an important preparation for her[19] later work, for she kept at work in the theater after this start. Yesterday I read a story about her in[20] the paper.

In a little city there lived a little fellow with a real love for machines. He read many books[21] on all subjects and prepared and published a paper which he would sell on the train where he kept his shop. Above all,[22] he was always a hard worker and worked many hours to finish something of importance. This lad was Thomas[23] Edison.

Let me tell you of another lad, a collector of books about the sea and a lover of the[24] company of either ships or sailors. This lad was John Paul Jones. He was taken into the home of a man named[25] Jones, the owner of a big country place, and Paul was very dear to his heart. Paul Jones was very daring and bore arms[26] for his country and brought honor to the flag. In his opinion nothing was of greater importance than his country.[27] He was regarded as a real hero and was given a cross by the French minister, an honor never[28] before given to others than Frenchmen.

Another lad, later to become a great worker for his fellow men,[29] was Mr. Peabody. When a small lad, his manners were good, in the opinion of his teachers, and he was[30] regarded with affection by them. They said he should go to college and study the subjects he liked so much, but he[31] left his books, as it was necessary for him to earn money. Recollecting his own desire for preparation[32] and study, he did not collect much capital later, but rather loved to give a good deal of help to other[33] folks.

Most of these children of yesterday kept at their books and their preparation because they loved their work so[34] much. These are but five of the many folks that have been of great help to their fellow men. (695 standard words)

Assignment 15

74. Day, dare, dares, many, manner, manners, ready, reader, readers, tea, tear, tears, owner, owners, sister, sisters, leader, leaders, chair, chairs.

75. Though, although, thought, throw, throat, author, both, health, these, theme, thin, thick, thicken, thickness, months.

76. *(a)* Concrete, confer, confess, conscience, convey, convince, consolation. *(b)* Compel, compensation, compress, compression, combat, compass, complex. *(c)* County, counties, counsel, counsellor, account.

77. *(a)* Fairly, briefly, chiefly, early, only, openly, plainly, rarely, safely, slowly, lately, mainly, calmly. *(b)* Gladly, greatly, mostly, orderly, partly, generally. *(c)* Easily, family, heartily, readily, hastily, merrily. *(d)* Totally, socially, locally, materially.

78. Reading Exercise

The Hermit

Jack is a hermit. He has no family and lives in a lonely cave. He seeks the company of no man or[1] woman, but goes calmly about his work. A visitor would see him early in the morning, with a thin robe thrown[2] about his back, seeking both herbs and flowers. You can see that he loves the black earth and the odor of growing things.[3]

He lives at peace with all living things and plans only good for his fellow men. The folks show their affection for him[4] by getting him fresh milk, although they cannot spare very much. They place the milk before his cave door. The hermit's conscience[5] compels him to give back these tokens of affection.

He goes about his work slowly but he is on the job[6] every day. Because of his great age, you would think that he would be ill, but he never misses a day.

Jack would not[7] kill any living thing. For months he lives only on berries. He eats no meat. He would never kill the rabbit that[8] lives in the grass near his cave. The sparrow need not leave hastily after taking a bit of bread, as the hermit[9] barely notices him. The hermit conveys the feeling that he is immensely happy when the rabbit or sparrow[10] makes a call. In the cave everything is almost in darkness. As the visitor becomes more at home, he sees[11] the cot and the bench with pots and pans on the floor. There is hardly more in the cave than one chair and one cot. A heavy[12] smoke floats to the ceiling where you see neat rows of herbs. There is an odor of herbs in the cave. It is a clean[13] odor. Jack confessed that he generally studied about herbs in his spare time. He knows everything about them.[14]

All the people in the country steadily come to see him about their ills and he helps them all, but they have very little[15] money. His consolation is that he made them happy by his good deed.

One chilly evening Jack[16] was sitting in his cave, stirring his pots of herbs and having a little tea. It was fairly early in the evening.[17] Then he heard screams. He could readily hear the screaming, even over the roar of the gale. Only a step or[18] so from his cave lay a man. He was bleeding from gashes made by a lance. His horse fell and his left leg was broken.[19] The hermit was very hardy, and it was no trick for him to get the man into the cave. The hermit could see[20] plainly that the man was wealthy.

After almost a month had passed, the hermit saw that the fever was gone and that[21] he was gaining steadily. His leg and arm were bound. He was pale and shaky after the fever. He was very[22] thirsty and wanted something to eat. He was soon able to talk and tell Jack what had taken place.

"I started from[23] Italy with many goods of real value. I was on the frozen road for many days. I was very thirsty[24] and wanted something to eat and a place to sleep, but there was no inn. Then some fierce men leaped from the dark road and knocked[25] me from my horse. That was when my leg was broken. They stripped me of all my money."

A little time after the wealthy[26] man heard of the hermit's death. It made him very sad. He went back over the same road to the cave, thinking it would[27] help him make a plan. He noticed that all the folks were sad. There was no more good hermit to help the sick. They missed the[28] aged man, tottering about with all his herbs. (568 standard words)

ASSIGNMENT 16

79. Either, loves, collected, companies, becoming, prepared, real-regard, wants, receives, situations, gladden, also, gives, got, next, presents, letter-let, morning, some, such, matters, parted, against, publishes, always, about them, very well, I should be, I have been, there has been, after, very truly yours, over, I could not, I did not, he would not, what was, into the, I can go, in the, I told, he told me, several days, upon the, if you would be, I have given, for these.

80. Dearly, daily, nearly, merely, likely, names, letters, families.

81. To own, to honor, to obey, to our, to like, to see, to say, to pay, to place, to believe.

82. As well as, as good as, as low as, as much as, as great as, as soon as.

83. Have been, I have been able, have not been able, I have not been able, would be able, I would be able, he would be able, they would be able, you would be able, should be able, you should be able, will be able, I will be able, you will be able, he will be able, may be able, I may be able, you may be able, he may be able, they may be able, to be able, has been able.

84. Send, agree, ask, office, official, future, special-speak-speech, week-weak, floor-flour, complete-complain-complaint, immediate-immediately, committee, represent, already, value, employ, express, knowledge.

85. Reading Exercise

JOAN OF ARC

If you have not already heard the story of the brave little girl, Joan of Arc, send for the book Mr. Paine wrote.[1] You should be able to place an order for it as soon as you get to the office. It is my opinion that[2] after reading it you, too, will be glad to tell it to others.

When Joan was a little girl, she lived in the country.[3] The real date of her birth is not known, but it is thought to be between 1410 and 1412.[4] Although her family's wealth was far from great, her folks were well known in that section of the country.

When she was[5] small, she was like most other children of her time. There was nothing special to mark her as one who would be able[6] to achieve great things in the future.

During the reign of Charles VI, the country was in the hands of two factions.[7] One faction had seized the Dauphin, as the heir to the French throne was known, but this faction soon released him. It was believed[8] by the people that their nation would be saved by a woman. Little Joan of Arc was always a dreamer. She[9] saw many visions. She was told that it was her task to help the Dauphin and save France. When she was nearly fifteen,[10] a vision came to her which she believed urged her to break the siege which the enemy had laid about the city.[11]

The Dauphin was a weak man, but he was her prince and it was necessary to gain his favor. Although she was[12] thoroughly convinced that she was chosen to take an important part in the cause of France, she was aware that she[13] must get the aid of the prince. Much time had already been lost. Immediately Joan went to the Dauphin. She was[14] dressed in men's clothing. He was willing to let her speak, so she was taken into his presence. She told the prince of[15] her visions and also expressed her desire to lead an attack upon the enemy.

Her story could not be[16] kept a secret. It was soon common knowledge in the market place. Men left their places of business and collected[17] in public places to tell what they heard regarding the girl and her mission. Many men believed her story. A[18] committee of men agreed that there was truth in her tale.

The city council gave her an army. She was seated[19] on a black horse clad in armor. She could employ no army tactics of any value because at no time did[20] she have a thorough knowledge of army methods. Her only thought was to attack the enemy as soon as it[21] was possible.

Her ardor was such that, with Joan as the leader, the French soldiers soon drove off the enemy. The[22] siege started and the city was saved. They won another victory and about three months later the prince, as well[23] as Joan and the army officials, rode into the city where the prince was made Charles VII of France.

When Joan[24] reached the age of seventeen her work for France had not yet been completed. Paris, as well as other parts of the[25] country, was in the hands of the enemy. In her visions Joan was still being urged to save France, but the orders[26] she got in her visions were very vague. She led the army in an attack upon Paris, but could not take the[27] capital city. Many people lost faith in her and wanted to give in to the enemy and some soldiers[28] would not obey her. Several of her comrades in arms went with her to relieve the situation in another[29] city to which the enemy had laid siege.

She was taken prisoner during this siege. From that time until[30] the hour of her death she was in a dirty prison. Week after week Joan had to live on a dirty floor, but she[31] made no complaint, even though she was often subjected to shame in every manner. At one time she nearly escaped[32] and after that she was placed in chains. The people thought that Charles would ransom her, but he forgot his debt to her.[33]

A committee representing the enemy was planning means of getting rid of her. The committee complained[34] that her visions were evil and not from heaven as was generally believed. She was bound to the stake and, amid[35] the flames, the little "Maid of France" bravely met her death. (710 standard words)

CHAPTER IV

Assignment 17

86. Motion, drove, fellow, brought, draw, salt, hot, block, sorrow, coal, ready, reader, readily, readers, own, only, owner, owners, to pay, as well as, would be able.

88. Who, to, do, tooth, food, fool, drew, shoot, boots, through, mood, canoe, noon, smooth, cool, choose, whose.

89. Cut, does, dozen, cup, up, us, cousin, rug, luck, utmost, production, reduction, none, numb.

90. Hook, took, pull, cook, foot, shook, sugar.

91. Reading Exercise

A Secret Vacation

As I started up the stairs, I took note of the dozens of jobs that had to be finished either that day or early[1] the next

morning. As I drew near the study hall, I shuddered because I was at the foot of my class in my[2] studies. Who would
not feel gloomy and jealous when his pals played football and
he did nothing but study? A group of[3] my buddies were
almost through with the work for the semester, but even
though I did my utmost, I could keep up[4] with none of them.

I did want so much to shut my dull books and play with
my buddies. If I could only shut my books[5] in the closet,
I would be happy, but I could not do this, so what was the
good of thinking about it?

My thoughts[6] were on food, and I did want to catch a
duck that my cousin could cook. As I would shoot the duck,
I would chuckle. With[7] these thoughts I sat on the bench
and did not want any more work. The urge to get loose from
my books was getting[8] greater and greater. But there must
be no fooling—I must get busy.

As I raised my head, I saw my teacher coming up[9] the row.
She took about three steps and before she put her left foot
on the rug again, she halted. At first, I was[10] utterly in
the dark as to what was going on. Then I noticed that the
murmurs of my classmates had ceased. The[11] cuckoo clock by
the stairs did not tick. Even my cousin who was sitting in
the stuffy hall too stared at me—or[12] at whom was he staring?
Immediately I took in the situation and left the group. By the
door lay my[13] poodle, with one paw raised. Everything was
very still. Then I saw that the spell was in the open as well
as in[14] the study hall. Many people were caught in the spell
of the cool air. A man was dusting his boots with a piece
of[15] cloth cut from a rug. Several small children had been
playing football and one was about to tuck the ball under[16]
his arm. A cashier was giving a reduction to a cautious girl.

What a week! I did nothing but fish every[17] day. The fish were foolish and bit on my hook.

Then I heard something like a roar and there I was sitting in my chair[18] in the study hall. The low roar grew heavier and then the spell was gone. I heard the bell which meant that the end of[19] the hour had come.

As I started on my trip home, I thought of all my good times and I felt so good that I was sure[20] I would soon lead all my classes. (405 standard words)

Dear Sir: Your letter of May 10 did not reach me until this morning. The dozen rugs mentioned in that letter were[1] not shipped because our production man was sick. A truck ran over his foot the day before yesterday and he has[2] been in the hospital ever since. These rugs should be ready soon, though, as we have taken on several other[3] men to see that the work is finished.

We shall do all we can to see that this does not happen again, but errors[4] and delays will creep through. Yours truly, (86 standard words)

Dear Sir: Your letter of May 21 reached me this morning. I shall see the man about whom you ask. I shall also[1] show him your letter if that plan suits you. Yours truly, (30 standard words)

ASSIGNMENT 18

92. Boat, boot, known, none, talk, took, draw, drew, hot, hut, lock, luck, cool, coal, loss, lose, pole, pull, blow, blue.

93. Care, carry, force, charge, look, clear, skill-school, usual-wish, govern-government, expect-especial, full, sure, number, enough, position, question, purchase, remember.

94. Reading Exercise

PRAIRIE SOD MANSIONS

There is no question that there are not many people today who care to hear very much about the log cabin[1] and who remember enough about it. The stories about the log cabin, and the important part it played in[2] the history of our government, are little known to a number of people.

The men who made their homes where there[3] were trees growing had merely to chop the trees and carry them to a spot that could easily be cleared. They did not[4] have to go far for such a spot.

The men who made their homes in the prairies did not have such an easy time. The first[5] settler who was forced to put up a sod home was looked upon as a real hero. After leaving everything[6] in the east that was near and dear and tramping over the great open spaces, he was in a sad position. As[7] he looked over his claim, he did not see a tree. When he left the east he did not expect to see many trees but[8] he thought surely that there would be a number of trees from which he could make a place in which to live. The early settler[9] could not purchase enough food such as bread, meat, and sugar even though he was willing to pay the charge for them,[10] as such food was hard to get.

As he could not make a log cabin and the government could do little for him, his[11] first thought was that he would live in a cave. After thinking the matter over fully, he changed his opinion. After[12] looking at the sod for a time, the early settler, showing clearly that there was no question about his skill,[13] set to work making a home from the sod.

It was clear to the settler that he needed only one acre for his[14] home and so with the aid of a team of horses he easily got this acre into good shape. He took especial[15] pains with this acre as he would surely be forced to live on it for many days. He was sure he could carry[16] the work to completion without taking too much time.

He took a sharp spade and with care chopped the sod into small sections.[17] As he was putting these sections into position, he remembered that he needed more tools, but as he could[18] not purchase them, he did without them.

As usual, his first thoughts were on an easy method to heat the place when[19] the snow fell. It was rather dark but he could not expect to have everything. His next task was to get his home full[20] of hay that would come in handy for heating purposes. He did not have to purchase the hay— there was no charge for[21] it!

After his home was completed, the settler's days were full. He was very busy preparing for the next season.[22] The settler was alone but for his little prairie dog who was always with him. The dog would carry his stick[23] but he would always remember to give it back after the two were through strolling. The little dog and the settler[24] often saw a number of rabbits and more than once had a feast on a rabbit who did not look where he was going.[25] Most of the rabbits, though, were sure-footed and hopped about rapidly, especially when they saw the settler[26] and his dog.

As the settler had a number of positions to fill, such as cook, maid, and cleaner, he arose very[27] early in the morning. When he got up, he could still see the stars, rapidly fading from the heavens. (558 standard words)

Dear Sir: Have you ever thought of going to evening

school? I know that you work hard all day and that you are not in[1] a mood for study when you are through. But I also know that you will not get an increase in your salary if[2] you sit back and do nothing.

Come to our evening school and study the subjects that will help you in your work. We give[3] a good business course and if you register you will never be sorry.

We charge very little for our full business[4] course and if you cannot pay the whole fee immediately, we shall be glad to wait until you can. Yours very[5] truly, (101 standard words)

Dear Sir: There will be a meeting of our committee on May 10. The purpose of the meeting is to get some money[1] to pay for the ball that we are planning in honor of the mayor. We have already collected a good[2] deal of money but we have far from enough.

I am going to ask the governor to be with us at this meeting[3] for I know he will be glad to help.

The mayor will be very happy when I tell him of our plans. Yours truly,[4] (81 standard words)

ASSIGNMENT 19

95. Charged, looked, clearing, schools, remembered, purchaser, enough, surely, full, positions, questioned, care, numbers, governments, asked, officials, complained, already, values, believed, wanted.

96. We, way, wait, waited, weed, weave, wave, wages, waste, weary, wheat, wheel, whale, wash, watch, wall, wool, swim, sweet, swift.

97. Quick, quit, dwell, queen, square, doorway, roadway.

98. Away, await, awaited, awake, awaken, ahead.

99. Reading Exercise

A Day to Remember

The whole school was waiting for the big football game that was to be played that afternoon. We won every game and wasted[1] no chance to get ahead of the other teams.

In the morning, there was a rally, with woolen banners waving,[2] and flags on the walls. Even the doorway and the roadway had flags. The people were whistling and hollering for the[3] team to win a quick victory.

Everyone was waiting in the hall when we heard the bell. Several of the stars[4] of our team were present on this morning. The leader called the meeting to order quickly. Everyone was awake[5] and watching. The first speaker was the coach who said that the team will not quit until it wins this important game. He[6] urged that everyone witness the game, wearing a woolen sweater if possible. No one should stay away. He spoke[7] of some of his games with teams that did not play fair and square. Before he finished, he gave the[8] names of all the players on the squad and the positions they would fill. As he called each name, he waved the player to[9] come quickly to the stage. There were many cheers and much whistling as the players went swiftly back to their seats. The cheer[10] leader called for three cheers for the coach and the whole squad.

A man who was in the hardware business and who never stays[11] away from a game was asked to speak. His talk was over quickly because when he was in school, he swore he[12] would make no speeches that would cause people to get weary. When he was eighteen, he left school so that he could become[13] a swimming teacher, but he loved football too, and hoped that when the whistle blew at the end of the game our team would[14] be far ahead. We are quoting from his talk in our school paper.

The cheer-leading squad of four girls walked on the stage[15] again and this time they wore woolen sweaters. Everyone was carried away by their vim and vigor. When the girls[16] urged every man and woman to go to the game, the number of tickets bought started to swell quickly. The school was[17] to be closed early that day and everyone was awaiting the bell.

Even the teachers thought of nothing but the[18] game. The history teacher did not give a quiz and waved the class on its way. The teachers hoped it would not rain because[19] the team could not play very well on the wet grass. When the whistle blew it was raining and one man said the only[20] way to get a score was to swim over the goal. There was only one real gain by our team, and that came near the end[21] of the game in the closing minutes of play when the left half-back crossed the goal. The score was six to nothing in our[22] favor and the whole school was hollering and whistling. This same half-back made a good kick and the score was then seven[23] to nothing—and that was the score at the end of the game. The whistle blew, and our team, wet and weary, ran into[24] the dressing room.

Football is a great game even when it is played in the rain. (493 standard words)

Dear Sir: We have your letter of May 11. We received the rates you quoted us for the suits which we shall need for the[1] coming holidays. There is one thing I must mention—although we need the goods immediately, we cannot pay[2] for them at this time. We shall do our utmost to pay for the purchases, but you must remember that we have had[3] to take care of a great many repairs to our shop. You are aware, though, that we have always taken care of our[4] debts.

We are going to save much money in the next month or two as we plan to reduce waste to the minimum[5] in our shop. Very truly yours, (105 standard words)

Assignment 20

100. Represented, gladly, stated, situations, parted, favored, tells, named, forgive, underneath, almost, matters, against, I have not been, if you will, for that, I told, I cannot believe, may be able, he will be able, to believe, I should be, I should have, from which the, to the, in the, by those, as great as, as good as, to collect, he told me, they received.

101. World, reply, word, body, duty, bring, house-whose, remark-room, fall-follow, accept-acceptance, gone, nature, suppose, whether, further, explain, particular, report.

102. Yawn, yacht, youth, yet, year, yellow, Yale, yard.

103. Ring, rink, rang, rank, sing, sink, sang, sank, ring, rang, wrong, sing, sang, song, ringing, singing, hanging.

104. *(a)* Unfair, unconscious, undo, unfasten, unfinished, unlikely, unsafe. *(b)* Increase, income, infer, inform, install, insane. *(c)* Envy, engine, engineer, enforce, enrich, engrave, enroll. *(d)* Emblem, embrace, embarrass, emperor, embark. *(e)* Impress, impression, impossible, impair, implore.

105. Reading Exercise

A Fable

One spring morning there came to the campus of a small

engineering school a lad by the name of Russell. The dean[1] explained that he was famous in many parts of the world for his football. There were many good reports and flattering[2] words in the daily papers about his work.

He made a hit with all the girls and usually there was a[3] group of pretty maidens following him in a body to the games. The girls would even sing songs for him, and the[4] singing would ring in his ears for many days. It will not be necessary to say that all the lads were jealous[5] of this youth. They did their utmost to impress the girls and embarrass the youth. They did their utmost to show the girls[6] that they possessed an infinitely greater knowledge and that Russell was unfair. They said further that he was yellow[7] and would not play through the whole football year.

The girls replied with a good-natured grin and accepted the remarks[8] without a word. They watched Russell play whether the team played at home or had gone to another city.

The other[9] lads employed every method they could think of to impress the girls. They gave up their incomes to take the girls to supper.[10] They gave banquets that they hoped would bring them favor. They wasted precious afternoons wading in the stream looking[11] for yellow water lilies to bring to the ladies. Then, I suppose to win the favor of the girls, they took them[12] in a row boat. They even drove them in their autos to an inn, but it was impossible to win them over.[13] The girls were particular, they said, and went back to their houses. The lads even sang to the girls, but the girls thought[14] it their duty to ask them to refrain, explaining that the singing increased their headaches.

All this time Russell remained[15] at his work. He wasted no time nor cash on the girls. He would study in his little house and make his reports[16] when they would fall due. He would work early and late. He was envied by all the athletes. He never cast a glance at[17] the girls, but yet the foolish maidens followed him and asked him to explain some particular plays that he made.

Soon[18] the other lads accepted their fate and gave up their foolish pranks. They did not embarrass Russell any more; they[19] did not impress the girls any more; they informed the world that they would give their time to work. The youths sang the song, "One[20] for all and all for one," and from that day had nothing to say to the girls.

The lads worked as hard at making goals as[21] they formerly worked in wasting their Dads' money. The lads were going to undo all the harm that their remarks and[22] actions had made. They accepted their duties good-naturedly, whether the duties were easy or impossible.[23]

After much work, with many a busy morning and evening, these lads, once Russell's inferiors, were soon as good[24] as he was in the game of football. One day, the lads were as famous as Russell. Then the girls were impressed,[25] particularly by the emblems the lads had won for their deeds in football. They yearned to be back with these lads and even[26] begged them to sing to them. The lads were not angry and, after all, "all is well that ends well!" (535 standard words)

ASSIGNMENT 21

106. Talk, solid, broke, brought, mop, chop, stuff, drug, sugar, foot, choose, dozen, wing, wink, swing, rang, rank, yard, yarn.

107. Examine, exceed, excess, expense, explode, expression, explore.

108. (*a*) Things, savings, readings, sayings, evenings, meetings, dealings, bearings. (*b*) Exceedingly, seemingly, willingly, knowingly, feelingly, unwillingly.

109. Unknown, unnoticed, unnecessary.

110. Long, among, young, yes, thank, effort, strengthstrong, communicate-communication, bill-built, friend-friendly, else-list, car-correct, character, effect, return, answer, experience, recent.

111. Reading Exercise

FURS

Among the people of this country there are not very many who know the part that furs have played in the recent[1] history of our country. The strong fur trappers played an important part in settling the country without the help[2] of good methods of communication.

About 1870, furs were rare in France and other countries. At[3] that time, beaver hats were in fashion but the fur for these hats was exceedingly hard to get. Great effort was put[4] forth to get furs for the French for this purpose.

In still earlier times, only kings and wealthy people could wear furs.[5] In France, the common people both young and aged had to wear clothes made from strong cloth. Elsewhere the people thanked the richer[6] classes for rags from which they could make clothes to wear on chilly evenings and mornings.

Experience shows that each time[7] a new world had been visited the desire for fur began. The ocean got to be a road for ships going and[8] returning from the new world even though sailors said that the sea was full of monsters and that any ship that stayed[9] a long time on the water would soon be dragged to an unknown place.

Wealthy men built ships and went to this new world. The[10] greed for furs and excessive riches took men all over the globe. The strong character of many men, though, was in[11] their favor.

France was the leading nation in getting furs and metals. The effect of France's work was felt in all[12] parts of the world. The French went through the woods of the Great Lakes and returned with many furs and much metal. The experience[13] of the French was that it was easier to get the furs than the metals so they went in for furs.

The trappers[14] living in the woods received their food and other things from the fur company for which they worked. The company[15] always answered their call for food and went to every expense to get it to them. At times, this was far from easy[16] as there were no cars on which to ship the food.

As there were no bills to pay, the trappers and their families lived[17] happily. These people were always singing songs and were friendly to any one who visited them. These people had[18] no fear of hard work.

Their food was exceedingly plain. This food was cooked over a camp stove. Though the food was plain, it[19] was wholesome, but what else could a hungry man wish? After a long, hard trip, these trappers would have dealings with the fur[20] company to see that their accounts were correctly kept and that all the furs they brought in were correctly listed.[21] Yes, these trappers were exceedingly cautious.

After exchanging greetings, these men returned home where there would be drinking[22] and eating. The young men and young ladies would sing and dance.

After being at home for a time the trapper is[23] glad to get back to the woods again. Many trappers worked for the same company year after year.

One fur company[24] was started by a friend of our family. This friend got to be very rich.

Cities soon took the place of these[25] little posts. Many great cities were once nothing but homes where trappers made their quarters. (515 standard words)

CHAPTER V

Assignment 22

112. Recently, experiences, answered, returns, effect, character, cars, lists, unfriendly, bills, communicate-communication, strength-strong, thank, yes, young, among, longing, reported, particularly, explanation, further, weather, supposed, nature, gone, accepts, following, remarks, houses, bringing, duties, body, words, replied, worlds, cared, carries, forced, charged, looked, clearly, schools, usually, governs, expected, fully, surely, numbers, positions, unquestioned, purchased, remembered, sending, asked, immediate-immediately, committees, offices, represented, officials, already, future, values, speaks, weeks, floors, complained, employed, expresses, knowledge, opinions, subjects, prepared, children, together, yesterday, necessary, important-importance, books, company-keep, real-regard, dear-deal, capital, collects, loved, rather, above.

113. Unit, cue, cute, acute, few, view, human.

114. Toy, oil, toil, soil, annoy, noise, voice, join.

115. Lie, apply, applies, applied, arise, price. tries, tried, climb, tie, tire, nice, nicely, nicer, sign, fine, vine, sight, fight, cry, cries, crime, cried.

116. Ounce, now, cow, scout, mouth, mouse.

117. Reading and Writing Exercise

A Toy Store

Now that the holidays are near, many people start to think of the toys they will get for boys and girls. Our store has[1] a whole floor for toys and you can buy things that we know your boy or girl will prize and enjoy playing with.

We have tried[2] to get in a supply of fine toys from all over the world. A few of our cute toys come from Troy and many dolls[3] that are almost human come from China. They cry and make cute noises as though someone were annoying them. The dolls[4] do not weigh more than a few ounces.

You really do not realize what the toy makers can do until you have[5] seen our well-supplied store with all these nice toys. Come in and make your choice now. You will get excited over the toys[6] when you view them.

We have tiny toys from France—toys so tiny that they cause a good deal of eye strain to the human[7] being that tries to put them together.

Our library section, with its many files full of white slips, is the next[8] place you should visit. In the library, there are books of all types, for both boys and girls. We have added a number[9] of new books for the boy scouts. Few people realize what a fine gift a book makes. I have made a vow to give a[10] few books each year to the boys I know. Come in and browse a bit in our library. There are fine armchairs in which you[11] can sit and read without the annoyance of people's voices. All we ask is that you try to handle the books with[12] care and not soil them.

We have no books on crime. We know that if boys and girls get the habit now of reading fine books[13] that habit will never die and the children will always see to it that they are supplied with at least a few good[14] books.

Our supply of scout books is complete. We also have here a supply of scout uniforms. A boy should have a[15] scout uniform when he and his scout friends make a campfire.

In another unit of our store, we have a toy theater.[16] The puppets talk in a high voice and the children get excited. You should see their faces shine and you should hear[17] the showers of applause. We have a white cow that goes over the moon. One boy enjoyed watching this white cow so much[18] that he cried when he was forced to leave. Some children come twice and even three times and we almost have to drive them from[19] the store.

We have almost every game of which the human brain can think. There is no question you can make a fine choice.[20] Few stores have so much to show you You will enjoy the friendly confusion and the eager, excited faces of[21] our small friends.

Every day at four, in the dining room, we have ice cream for the children.

Let me guide you through our store.[22] Only in that way will you realize what a fine choice you can make.

Toys were meant not only for children but for[23] grown-ups as well. A man should always have time to play. The harder a man works, the more time he should take for play.

A[24] fine pastime for the business man is ice skating. After a hard day's work at the office, there is nothing[25] more satisfying than to pick up your skates and glide over the smooth ice of some adjoining lake.

Our store has given[26] a whole floor to skates. You will be able to get a pair of skates that will fit you perfectly. We know our skates[27] will help you enjoy to the fullest your days of skating on the frozen lake. Skates also make a fine birthday gift.[28] (560 standard words)

Assignment 23

118. Few, fuel, futile, youth, views, units, boil, choice, coil, moist, dime, files, slice, plow, arouse, rout, brow.

119. Life, line, quite, might, use, power, why, night, find, light, how-out, right-write, while, behind, point-appoint, thousand, side, wire, kind, inquire-inquiry, mile, require, lightly, kindly, rightly, nightly.

120. Reading and Writing Exercise

Greece

Thousands of years have gone by since Greece was considered a world power. Many have inquired why it was that these Greeks[1] could make such a mark on the world that we still remember and honor them. The man who studies Greek history might[2] inquire into the doings of these Greeks and find out why and how they got their power. Perhaps I should point out that this[3] inquiry might easily take a lifetime.

While we know something of the doings of the Greeks, I need not point out[4] that much truth about these people has yet to be brought to light. Often people find many objects, after digging[5] for quite a long time, that tell a little of the early life of the Greeks. They find coins and pins made from fine metal[6] wire as well as many kinds of jewelry. For thousands of years these things might have been under the earth, side by side,[7] and what a thrill it is to find these things.

While we are not able to say very much about Greek history, we[8] know that Troy was an important city. Outside the city of Troy, there were many miles of high walls. Every night[9] the Greeks would retire behind these miles of walls. A number of men were appointed to be outside the wall each night[10] to watch for the enemy.

History inquires into many things. History tries to find out why Athens was[11] a city of thinkers and people with great regard for the rights of others, while the people from other parts of[12] Greece were fighters. History tries to find out why our thought today does not seem to be quite as high as the thinking[13] of the Greeks.

The Greeks ate lightly. One would think that so strong a race would require much food of the right kind to keep healthy.[14] Their chief food was black soup.

Greece gave to the world a long line of great men. One great man to whom any good Greek will[15] point is Socrates. He was always trying to find that which was right and good. He believed that a spirit was behind[16] him that pointed out what he should do and how he should do it. He loved knowledge and asked about the use of almost[17] everything he saw.

The Greeks were quite happy when at play. The Greeks were famous for their games. The victors in the[18] games did not receive money but were given an olive wreath, which was lightly placed on their heads. The victors were honored[19] and thousands of people cheered from every side of the arena as they passed. The great writers of the day would[20] write poems about the victors and many of the lines they wrote are quite well known to the school children of today.

The[21] plays of Greece were also famous. Thousands of people would come from miles and miles, and stay in line, one behind the other,[22] while waiting their chance to get into the theater. The plays were given nightly. The players wore light masks that were[23] tied on with strong wire. The chorus that would sing at the beginning and at the end of the plays was required to be[24] behind the scenes.

The Greeks gave a prize to the man writing a good drama. The Greeks worked hard to win these prizes. When[25] a drama was produced by the players, the writer would look on and help as much as he could. Many fine plays that[26] these Greeks wrote are still given in our theaters today. I know you would enjoy seeing these plays as much as the Greeks[27] did when the plays were first put on. (545 standard words)

ASSIGNMENT 24

121. As well as, as great as, I would be able, he should be able, to obey, as many as, I cannot believe, I have told, I received, to form, to have, in which, of which, to which, life, rightly, lightly, thousand, wire, mile.

122. Signs, science, riot, prior, diet, via, lion.

123. Piano, mania, serial, create, creation.

124. Theory, genius, tedious, idea, ideal, quiet, new, renew, amuse, avenue, music, reduce.

125. Dollar, object, strange, trust, mail, address, respect-respectful-respectfully, arrange-arrangement, consider-consideration, across, opportunity, throughout, advantage, please, progress, various, enclose, wonder.

126. Reading and Writing Exercise

Money

We shall now consider money in its various shapes and forms. We shall consider it all the way from its early[1] stages right up to our present dollar. Please remember that money played as important a part in the[2] history of human progress as music or art. The men who saw the various advantages of money and[3] created a means with which people had an opportunity to buy and sell were gifted with genius. Today[4] we have an ideal means in the form of the dollar.

Prior to the use of the dollar, men used strange objects as[5] money. I wonder what the mail man would say today if we enclosed those same objects in our letters when paying[6] a debt. He would have a tedious task before him, carrying his heavy bag up the avenue and[7] delivering the mail to the various addresses. Wouldn't it be amusing to open our morning mail[8] and find a lion's skin as payment for a piano. As the lion's skin lay stretched out across our desk, we would[9] most likely lose five years' growth.

Throughout the ages, money has had an opportunity to play a great part. Prior[10] to the creation of money, people had strange ideas and theories about value. They felt that coins had no[11] particular value, and they gave them no respect and placed no trust in them.

Today we have new theories about[12] money. We have made arrangements to reduce the weight of the various objects that we use as money. Throughout[13] the business world, people take advantage of checks and other papers that have been created for business men. A[14] business man would not put coins or other forms of cash in a letter. He would sign his name to a check, put it in[15] an addressed letter and mail it. If the check is lost, he quietly makes another one. We think nothing now[16] of sending huge sums of money via the mails. The check is a sign of the great progress man has made. The science[17] of money has been studied by many great men.

One advantage of using precious metal as money is that[18] it is hard to get. If, through some wonder of science, the objects that represent our money should become easy[19] to get, then we should have to change to something else to represent our money. Men have tried for years to arrange some[20] way by which they could create precious metals. It is a tedious job, but men with a mania for precious[21] metals have put in renewed effort along these lines.

Please do not consider money as wealth. You may have wealth in[22] the form of cattle, horses, and other objects. Money alone has no value if there is no opportunity[23] to use it. We have no respect for the miser who is always on a diet in order to save dollars.[24]

In the days of the Greeks, when metal was used for money, it was necessary to arrange to carry huge money[25] chests from place to place, as there were no checks to take care of this tedious task. Robbers would often stay in the[26] woods and steal these chests from the coaches as they went across the country. Thousands of dollars in precious metals, enclosed[27] in strong chests, were stolen in this way. There were many riots throughout the country when these stage coaches carried[28] precious metals.

In early times governments had to deal with people who made money by various means. Some men[29] would chip off bits from the coins. Others would put the coins in a sack and shake the coins. Then they would pick up the chips and[30] make them into new coins. The government soon put an end to this. (611 standard words)

ASSIGNMENT 25

127. Rock, occur, lock, caution, arrow, slow, fur, drug, cook, fruit, tools, food, viewed, now, powder, try, type, join, toil, boy, advantages, pleased, various, opportunities, objected, trusted, respected.

128. Sun, fun, funny, summer, run, come, begun, lunch, luncheon, lumber, crush, touch, rush, judge, brush, blush, town, down, brown, drown, crown.

129. Assume, resume, consume, presume, assumption, resumption, consumption, presumption.

130. Reading and Writing Exercise

NORWAY

In Norway, the sun stays up until ten every night during the summer. It is no presumption to say that you[1] could easily read a book on the porch of your bungalow up to that time. As you get near the Arctic region,[2] the sun stays up all night. A part of the sun may be seen all the time. This would be a funny thing to see and it[3] would be fun to live in such a country in the summer.

Big cakes of ice float about in the sea. These cakes are so[4] big that they could easily crush a ship and drown everyone on that ship. Tons and tons of ice lie about in big[5] chunks. You can judge from this that it is hard to explore these regions and I assume you have heard of the many deaths[6] that have been announced.

Many people come to visit this region during the summer. They bring their trunks and stay to enjoy fishing for brown trout, as they listen to the rush of water in the icy streams.

There is a touch of[8] magic about the whole country. A man can drown his sorrows looking at the huge trees that will some day be cut down[9] and made into lumber. Norway consumes very little lumber and it is safe to assume that most of it is[10] for outside consumption.

The Vikings add a touch of romance to the history of Norway. They loved to sail the[11] seas in their ships and had no fear of drowning. They went to France, resumed their sailing, and then went to Italy. No[12] one could harm them, or run down their ships. At that time, the Vikings were feared by all the towns that lay by the sea. The Vikings[13] would rush upon the town and steal everything in sight. Great sums of money were brought back to Norway.

History[14] tells us that their ships touched the shores of this country in the year 1000. We assume that they made many trips but[15] we have no record to which we can refer.

Along the shores of the sea we find many fishing and lumbering[16] towns. Millions of fish are caught and consumed by the people of Norway. Every summer the men rush out and catch millions[17] of herrings. These fish are salted and dried in the sun. Some are served fresh at luncheon. These fish are also shipped to[18] France and other countries for consumption.

The visitor in Norway can have a good deal of fun. A person can[19] go skating or skiing at almost any hour of the day. It is nothing to run from one town to another[20] on skates. If you have a gun, you can go up among the pine trees and catch some game for luncheon. Some hearty folks even[21] go swimming but they rush from the water soon after they jump in. After a swim, the people resume their work,[22] if they have not caught pneumonia!

The ruler of Norway wears a crown. We can assume that the people of Norway[23] live a quiet life and do not try to put aside their king.

In the summer, you may see the hay drying in the[24] valley. There is a good deal of rushing to get the hay in on time.

As I said, there is a touch of romance about[25] the whole country. When the summer is gone, you will not like to pack your trunk and go home. You will feel that your[26] vacation and fun have only begun. But the boat will not wait, though, and you must say good-bye to the country in which[27] the midnight sun hangs over the sky. (545 standard words)

ASSIGNMENT 26

131. Throughout the, to consider, to return, among the, to correct, to report, send the, you will be able, to like, as much as, you should be able, upon them, I have read, I told, with the, I cannot, as well as, I did not, he would not, to plan, to be.

132. (*a*) Permit, perform, performance, perhaps, pursue, persuade, persuaded. (*b*) Promote, promotion, profession, promise, proper, approach, provision.

133. Sensible, available, humble, reliable, table, terrible, valuable, respectable, remarkable, favorable, answerable.

134. Simple, sample, ample, example, scruple, disciple.

135. Reading and Writing Exercise

The Power of a Smile

A smile is like the summer sunshine. Perhaps we have all felt the truth of that remark. A smile requires so little[1] effort, yet it is our most valuable asset. No matter what profession you pursue, a proper and[2] appropriate smile will help you win a promotion. I know you have seen many examples of this.

We all know[3] how much we like a man who greets us with a sunny smile. We immediately feel better for having met him,[4] no matter how humble or respectable he may be. This feeling remains with us and we pass it on to the[5] next man we meet. We have seen the remarkable power of a smile to crush a terrible anger. We have seen[6] a smile take much of the bitterness out of harsh and perhaps ill-chosen words.

When things annoy us, why do we not[7] rise above our simple feelings and permit a smile to creep across our faces? Perhaps the most reliable[8] sign of a great man is his power to refrain from being annoyed by petty things. The simple, unreliable[9] man is sure to be annoyed when he is approached for the smallest favor. A smile should be his most valuable[10] asset but he cannot take this sensible view.

There are people who rarely permit a smile to approach their[11] lips. Life seems to have little for them, either in the way of ample promotion or happiness. Misery and[12] trouble seem to pursue them and they have no time available for good cheer. If these people would only try to[13] smile at their troubles, they would find ample time for play.

A smile is always a good risk and one that pays well. It takes[14] little persuasion to be convinced that there is profit in a grin. The sight of a smiling face approaching will[15] give new hope to those who are tired from the strife of the world.

How terrible it would be for all of us if we could[16] not smile properly! We have said nothing thus far of the brave and noble smile that hides some terrible grievance. Very[17] often a man will grin while his real thoughts make him miserable. A man who can be persuaded to smile when[18] he is down and out is an example of a fine and noble character.

"Smile and the world smiles with you; weep and[19] you weep alone" is a saying that is perhaps known to more people than any other saying. The world is always[20] looking for sensible, reliable men but no man, no matter how valuable he may be or how[21] much promise he may show, will really enjoy life properly if he cannot smile and brush away his troubles.

The[22] power of a smile has made a smooth path for many great men. (440 standard words)

Dear Sir: I should like to use a few boys in our store for filing letters. If it is possible, I should like to[1] get boys who have some idea of our business. I will need those boys immediately.

We wish only the right kind[2] of boy to apply. We plan to promote these boys as soon as there is an opening.

Please write me if you know of[3] someone for this position. Yours very sincerely, (69 standard words)

Dear Sir: We have your letter regarding the white signs which you say you have not yet received. After looking through our[1] shipping files, we note that the signs in question were shipped to you on May 18. The signs should have reached you long before[2] this time.

We shall try to find these signs by tracing them from the shop. If we cannot find them, we shall make up new ones[3] for you.

Please write me if you receive them during the coming week. Yours truly, (73 standard words)

ASSIGNMENT 27

136. Enclosed, wonders, various, pleases, advantageous, opportunities, objected, addresses, mails, trusting, stranger, answers, character, listed, strongly, yes, among, long, efforts, replies, bringing, remarkable, followed, acceptable, supposed, explanation, forced, numbers, purchases, fully, clearly, questioned, sending, officials, immediate-immediately, valuable, employer, collectible, necessarily, subjects, situations, courses, purposes, wanted.

137. Treatment, amusement, excitement, moment, enjoyment, payment, agreement, apartment, statement, shipment, appointment, employment.

138. Problem, success, probable, except, stop, accord, person-personal, regret-regular, confident-confidence, correspond-

correspondence, excel-excellent-excellence, organize-organization, perfect-proof, satisfy-satisfactory, bed-bad, cover; serious, direct.

139. Reading and Writing Exercise

THE MAN ON HORSEBACK

How was it that a little person like Napoleon, brought up on a tiny island off the coast of Italy,[1] could excel every one else and direct the affairs of nations? There were five sons in Napoleon's family[2] but there is no proof that any of the other sons met with any particular success in life. We are[3] satisfied that while Napoleon was Emperor his treatment of his family was excellent. He gave them[4] many appointments, if we are to believe the statements that occur in his correspondence.

Napoleon's[5] family had little money and it was a serious problem for his folks to send him to school. We regret that[6] Napoleon's life at school was far from a happy one. According to reports, the boys were cruel in their treatment[7] of Napoleon and he could not stop them. He was a haughty lad and was confident he could be a success[8] even though he possessed a bad impression of most of the boys in the school. Napoleon probably got the[9] most enjoyment out of reading books about Julius Caesar.

He loved history and science and got amusement[10] and excitement by organizing plans with toy soldiers. People were in agreement that he did not have any[11] love for the finer things of life but he did try to write a book once. Though it was considered satisfactory,[12] it was by no means a work that a person would read from cover to cover. I am confident, though, that one can[13] get an excellent knowledge about Napoleon as a person by reading this book.

As a young man, his manners[14] were bad and often were the cause for serious thought on the part of his folks. He was eager to solve any[15] and all problems and he asked many questions even though some were cause for amusement. His clothing, except for a[16] new hat that he bought, was badly mended and the boy had to cover a hole in his shoe with a regular piece[17] of paper.

When he was wealthy and success had knocked at his door, he stopped at nothing to satisfy his desire[18] for fine garments. A shipment of fifty new suits which he picked out personally was quite a usual occurrence,[19] according to his friends.

As a youth, he received a small appointment in the army and the confidence with[20] which he took the appointment was proof that he was eager to see action. He was far from satisfied with his lot,[21] as he did not care to obey orders and take directions. He was far from a perfect soldier and overstayed[22] his leave many times.

An excellent opportunity came to Napoleon one day and he took advantage[23] of it. The French Directory remembered his fine work and called him to France to stop the enemy when the[24] Directory was being seriously attacked. Napoleon was made leader of the army in Italy.[25] He immediately started organizing the troops and did not stop until he was satisfied that they were[26] in perfect order.

The manner in which Napoleon escaped harm was remarkable. He was probably in[27] the open more than any of his soldiers yet, except for a few scratches, he was never hit by a shell.[28]

Napoleon said he was confident he would never get trapped in Russia, but Russia was the beginning of his[29] undoing. He followed the enemy, which kept falling back before him. The enemy then set fire to its cities[30] so that there was no food for Napoleon's army. It was a sad army that came back to France. Napoleon's[31] star was slowly setting.

Later he went to Elba, and then to Waterloo. Those were cruel years for the former[32] Emperor. His jailer watched him closely. Napoleon was a sick man and he tried to pass the hours away by[33] writing about his experiences. In 1821, he died and was buried under a willow tree[34] near his prison home. The grave was soon covered with weeds because of lack of care. (693 standard words)

CHAPTER VI

Assignment 28

140. Human, unit, voice, join, tire, sign, tried, ounce, cow, lightly, finds, lines, thousands, wires, permit, terrible, treatment, example, performance.

141. Own, owned, sign, signed, strain, strained, join, joined, print, land, planned, plenty, apparent, around, refund, sound, found, sent, front, event, prevent, inventory.

142. Seem, seemed, trim, trimmed, blame, blamed, claim, claimed, prompt, empty, remedy, framed, ashamed.

143. Reading and Writing Exercise

Dear Sir: I received your letter of May 16 in which you say that you desire to rent the two vacant lots owned[1] by my client, Mr. Trent. Thank you for your prompt reply.

Mr. Trent was in this city yesterday and it was[2] my good luck to run into him. While we dined, I outlined your plan and he seemed very much impressed. He was glad that[3] you planned to improve the land by planting a flower bed on it, as this will not only be an asset to the[4] other surroundings but it will save him the trouble of hunting for a man to cut the weeds every summer.[5]

Apparently, though, Mr. Trent cannot complete the deal alone. I found out that before this land can be rented all[6] the papers must be sent to his aunt to be signed. His aunt is joint owner with Mr. Trent. Mr. Trent is confident,[7] though, that his aunt will give her consent. If you will call at my office in about a week, I think I shall be[8] able to tell you if you may rent this land. Cordially yours, (170 standard words)

Dear Sir: Mr. Bond, the mayor of this town, has recently signed a five-year lease on a house that I have owned for[1] more than six months. The house has been empty for all that time and I must have it cleaned and painted before he moves in.[2] I would be ashamed to rent the house in its present state.

I have been looking around for a man who could do this[3] work properly and promptly and your name was suggested. I wonder if you would consent to take charge of putting[4] the house and the grounds in perfect order. As I said, the house has been vacant for six months, and during this time the[5] boys in the surrounding blocks have harmed the grounds a good deal. Apparently, the parents of these boys had not trained them[6] to stay away from empty houses.

I made an inventory of the things that I will have to buy before Mr.[7] Bond moves in, and I found that there were only three or four things that had to be bought. If Mr. Bond is well[8] satisfied, he may consider buying the house.

I have outlined everything that will have to be taken care of. First,[9] there is a hole in the roof. The other night it rained violently. The water came right through the roof and almost[10] ruined the ceiling in the bedroom. This situation will have to be remedied before we do anything else.[11] Then the whole house should be painted with a good brand of paint.

If you consent to take this job, please write me immediately.[12] I should like the work to be started on Monday, if possible. Although there is plenty of time, it is[13] important that these repairs be completed before winter sets in. Cordially yours, (275 standard words)

Dear Madam: At a meeting in February, we planned to put on a three-day sale of ladies' garments. We have[1] picked November as the month of the sale.

If you need a winter coat or a new dress, come to our store— we know you[2] will find something that will suit both your fancy and your purse.

We have never had a finer lot of coats at such low[3] prices. We have about fifty fur coats representing the season's most stylish models. If you dreamed of possessing[4] such a fine fur coat this winter, come in and see what we have to show you.

Our line of dresses is complete. We[5] have printed a book showing this year's styles. The style book is on its way to you and should reach you soon. When it comes, open[6] it to page

12 and examine the model shown there. This model was planned by a man who for ten years designed[7] dresses in well-known dress shops of France.

Visit our store and look at the many fine garments we have here. Yours truly,[8] (160 standard words)

ASSIGNMENT 29

144. Problem, stop, person-personal, direct, regret-regular, cover, serious, I will not, I may have, I wish, on this, under the, that it is, to give, you have not, I should be, as well as, we feel, to sell.

145. Fail, failed, field, filed, old, gold, child, held, sold, appealed.

146. Sunday, Monday, Tuesday, Wednesday, Thursday, Friday, Saturday, January, February, March, April, May, June, July, August, September, October, November, December.

147. Entire, copy, stock, stand, allow, draft, refer-reference, remit-remittance, suggest-suggestion, individual, attention, acknowledge, receipt, unable, enable, invoice, industry, oblige.

148. Reading and Writing Exercise

A BIRTHDAY PARTY

On Sunday, December 25, Mary would be eight years old. Her parents were not rich, but they owned a good house.[1] Her Dad was an important individual in the lumber industry, and lumber dealers would always pay[2] attention to his suggestions.

Mary was an only child and was a little spoiled, but she held a profound respect[3] for her parents and always yielded to their wishes. As Mary would be eight years old soon, her parents were going[4] to give her a party.

This appealed to Mary and she immediately started to form a list of the friends[5] she would ask. Mary made a rough draft, but had to acknowledge that she was unable to put all her friends on the[6] list and she could not stand leaving any of them off.

Mary was obliged to take a copy of her list to her[7] aunt and ask her what she should do. Her aunt suggested that she ask all the children who did not have a happy home,[8] as they would enjoy it most. Mary was sold on this idea and on Monday she made a list and sent a note to[9] each of the names on that list.

Mary said she did not want any presents but instead she wanted to purchase presents[10] for her guests. Her parents enabled her to carry out this plan and gave her the necessary money. She[11] was allowed to buy all the presents. She remitted promptly and received a receipt in return.

The party was[12] to be held at six in the evening. The morning was cold and the afternoon was even colder, but when the time[13] came the entire list was represented and everyone filed merrily into Mary's house.

At first all of them[14] seemed embarrassed, but Mary treated them so well that soon every individual was entirely at his ease.[15]

The guests filed into the dining room and were allowed to eat all they could. After everyone had dined, the doors of[16] the front parlor were thrown open and standing in the middle of the room was a big tree covered with lights. On the[17] top of the tree a gold star was fastened. A big bag of presents was pulled out from under the tree. The guests were[18] unable to thank Mary enough for her kindness. (368 standard words)

Dear Sir: Enclosed you will find copies of our invoices for March, April, May, and June. As you have not acknowledged[1] receipt of these invoices or the many letters we sent you, we assume you failed to receive them or else did[2] not pay any attention to them.

If it is impossible for you to send us a remittance immediately[3] to cover these invoices, please oblige us by signing a note and mailing it today. If we do not[4] receive this note, we shall have to refer this account to the man who has charge of collections. Sincerely yours, (99 standard words)

Dear Sir: Thank you for your remittance by draft for $98.75 in payment of your[1] September and October invoices. We regret we are unable to fill your entire order at this time.[2] We do not have in stock several of the individual parts for the machinery, but the factory[3] has promised to supply us, either on Thursday or Friday, with all the necessary parts.

I have referred your[4] letter of July 1 to the factory, and I know that will spur them on to give immediate attention[5] to this order.

Thank you again for remitting so promptly. The prompt settlement has enabled us to take care[6] of our own obligations. Yours truly, (127 standard words)

Dear Sir: The book on marketing mentioned in your letter of August 8 was sent to you on June 16. We[1] cannot explain why you have failed to receive it. We are mailing you another copy of the book immediately.[2] We are taking no chances on having the book go astray this time and we are sending it by[3] registered mail.

With the book you will also find a copy of the book on sell-

ing that we are publishing in[4] September. We know you will
enjoy reading it. Please accept it with our compliments. Yours
truly, (96 standard words)

ASSIGNMENT 30

149. Entirely, stocks, allowable, referred, suggestions, ac-
knowledgment, enables, invoices, probably, organized, director,
seriously, appointment, arrangements, objected, considers, addresses, enclosure, wonders, advantages.

150. *(a)* Gentle, genteel, regent, pageant, legend. *(b)*
Opened, happened, expend, ripened, cheapened, carpenter.

151. *(a)* Native, captive, motive, positive, sensitive. *(b)*
Defy, define, defeat, defend, defer, defraud. *(c)* Divide, division, devise, devote, devoted, endeavor.

152. Gentlemen, Dear Mr., Messrs., yours sincerely, sincerely
yours, very sincerely, yours very sincerely, yours respectfully,
respectfully yours, cordially yours, yours cordially.

153. Reading and Writing Exercise

JOHN SMITH AND THE NEW WORLD

John Smith was a native of the British Isles. When he was
fifteen his one desire was to devote his life to the[1] sea. He ran
away from home, wandered about the world and had many
narrow escapes and more than once was saved from[2] impend-
ing death. Finally, while defending his country against the
Turks, he was taken captive and sold as a[3] slave. His owner
was far from gentle with him, and one day Smith killed the
man and escaped.

He happened to reach home at[4] the very time that parties were being formed to go to the New World. Smith was always looking for something exciting,[5] and he eagerly joined a group that was leaving in December, 1606.

The colony was[6] made up of men unfitted for the work before them. Most of them were of gentle birth and had never completed[7] a day's work in their lives. Their motive for coming was to find gold and other valuables and then return home.[8] There was no carpenter or skilled laborer among them.

Smith endeavored to find a spot on which to settle that[9] would be easy to defend against the Indians. He was positive his people would have trouble with the natives.[10] He spent many days in this work. He was the only leader with any initiative in the group. Most of[11] the men deferred to his judgment. Several of them, though, endeavored to seize the only ship and return home. Smith[12] spent every effort to prevent them from doing this. When he opened fire on them, they gave up. One day Smith was[13] made a captive by the Indians. He devised many ways of amusing them and they treated him kindly. Smith[14] found out that the natives wanted him to be their leader and form a plan by which the Indians could break through the[15] defense of the white colony. When he defied them they placed his head on a block and were going to kill him, pending[16] the word of the chief. At this moment the chief's daughter rushed to the prisoner, threw her arms around his neck and begged for his life. History does not give her motive for doing this.

The little girl, who was about twelve years old[17] at that time, was always a friend of the white people after this and some years later she married a white[18] settler.

One year the food supply was very low and Smith found it necessary to ask the help of the Indians.[19] But the natives remembered how the white people defrauded them and laid a plot to kill Smith and his men.[20] This plot was defeated by Smith, who seized the chief, held a pistol to his head and said, "Grain or your life." We are told that[21] they got grain and plenty of it.

Smith now set the men to work. Dividing them into two groups he set one division[22] to work planting grain and the other division cutting lumber. Many tried to escape the labor, but Smith[23] threatened that if they did not work they would not eat—and all of them worked! (472 standard words)

Dear Mr. Brown: The carpenter in charge of repairing the woodwork in our building tells me that the metal[1] in your nails has been cheapened. He opened a keg of the nails and found hundreds of rusty ones. He divided the[2] good ones from the bad and is returning to you those which are not fit for use. He says that this happened once before[3] and that if it occurs again he will ask me to place the order with another company.

I realize[4] that once in a great while every organization will make an error, but when errors occur so often I[5] think you should start putting your house in order. Cordially yours, (110 standard words)

ASSIGNMENT 31

154. Signed, strained, rent, refund, blind, apparent, seemed, trimmed, blamed, remedy, framed, seriously, directly, regretted, successes, organized, badly.

155. Move, agent, spirit, credit, appear, beauty, differ-different-difference, approximate, deliver-delivery, instant-instance, response-responsible, rule-railway, quality, definite, tomorrow, influence, mistake-mistaken, altogether.

156. Reading and Writing Exercise

ROBIN HOOD AND HIS MERRY MEN

Robin Hood was a mere lad when he was fascinated by the beauty of the woods. He influenced others to[1] join him until his devoted followers numbered over 120. They defied the laws of the[2] country and robbed those who passed their way. The sheriff and his men tried many different ways to catch Robin Hood and[3] deliver him to the county jail, but their plans always met with defeat.

Robin seemed to have his agents in all[4] parts of the country, for it appears that he knew of everything that was going on. Although he was a bandit,[5] we must credit him with many fine qualities. One of his fine qualities, for instance, was shown by his rule that[6] no women should ever be harmed.

Robin married a girl who possessed not only great beauty but a strong character[7] as well. They lived very happily. I think it is safe to say that their happiness had a great influence[8] on bringing about the wedding of Alan and Ellen, two staunch followers of Robin.

As the days went on, the[9] king's spirits grew lower and lower because he thought Robin would never be caught. He called in one of his agents[10] and said, "Tomorrow you leave with fifty men. If you move cautiously, you should be able to catch this fellow and[11] deliver him to the sheriff." The king was mistaken. Even though the agent moved cautiously, he could not outwit[12] Robin, who took definite steps against having anything like this happen. Later Robin set the agent[13] and his men free on the promise that they would be responsible for paying a definite sum of money each[14] year, which was to be divided among Robin and his merry men.

Several weeks later, Robin heard that the[15] bishop was coming. His men dressed as sheep herders and camped at the edge of the woods. While waiting, they roasted a duck.[16] As the duck was roasting, the bishop came along, and being very hungry, he ordered his men to seize the meat,[17] which happened to be of fine quality. In an instant Robin blew his trumpet and got his men together. The[18] bishop was indeed amazed when he was taken prisoner. He, too, was released on his definite promise to[19] deliver to Robin a huge sum of money.

Some years later the ruler of the country pardoned Robin and[20] his men and asked them to spend their remaining days with him. They stayed for a while but were not altogether happy[21]—they longed for the great outdoors. One by one the men ran away and returned to the woods. Robin, too, lived his final[22] days in the woods that he loved so well. (446 standard words)

Dear Sir: In response to your recent letter of April 16, I think it is altogether apparent that[1] the agent in question has not been fair with the creditors. He gave a definite promise to deliver the[2] goods approximately February 3. Not only did he fail to deliver the goods, but he was indifferent[3] to the appeals of his creditors in failing to respond to their inquiries.

Fairness is a quality[4] that seems entirely lacking in the character of this agent. He does not have the qualities one should[5] possess in so responsible a position. I think it is a mistake to let him have our business.

It is my[6] thought that he should be removed by the railway company and a responsible agent put in his place. I shall[7] use my influence to bring this about. Yours truly, (149 standard words)

Gentlemen: I am glad that your frank letter of August 3 gives me an opportunity to explain our charge[1] of $7.50 for the cut made for your ad in the July issue of the "Industrial[2] Weekly."

Upon receiving your letter, we immediately checked our records and found that $7.50[3] was the price of the cut to our firm.

As we wrote you on June 17, we are willing to have our[4] clients supply us with their own cuts. We supply cuts when our clients ask us to, but we make no profit on this[5] end of our business.

Many of our friends want us to supply the cuts because it saves time and trouble. They also[6] find that their ad presents a better appearance when the cuts are made by our engravers, who have had years of[7] experience in this type of work.

We do hope that the appearance of your ad pleased you and that you will write me[8] again when I may help you in any way. Cordially yours, (170 standard words)

ASSIGNMENT 32

157. Allowed, industries, obligation, individually, copies, entirely, stands, attention, receipts, stopping, personally, according, problems, covered, shipment, trusted, considered, pleased, returning, answerable, recently, character, carries, numbered, purchaser, remembered, surely, government.

158. *(a)* Beneath, betray, below, begin, began, belong. *(b)*

Debate, depress, depression, depart, depend, deceit, decision. *(c)* Displace, disgrace, dispatch, discover, discredit. *(d)* Misplace, mishap, misgovern, misprint. *(e)* Repair, resign, resume, review, replace, revise, reform.

159. I had, they had, we had, she had, he had, you had, who had.

160. Reading and Writing Exercise

Dear Mr. Lee: In July, when I left for Maine, I had not planned to resume my duties as department head in[1] your organization. When I resigned at that time it was my impression that I would be replaced by the man[2] who had worked with me from the day I displaced Mr. Jones. As you know, Mr. Jones was dismissed because of the disgrace[3] he brought to the company.

I was so amazed to find Mr. Jones back at his old post that I have reconsidered[4] my decision to resign and plan to be at my old desk on Wednesday morning.

I cannot yet see why[5] this man who betrayed his company should be given this responsible position. The success of the company[6] depends very much upon the way this department is handled, and if we had Mr. Jones as the head, we[7] might get into trouble.

My first problem on Wednesday will be to review without delay all the revisions that[8] were made in prices. As you know, the prices were changed without debate when the depression came, but I think many[9] decreases may be made. Yours truly, (186 standard words)

Dear Sir: The printer was depressed—he had misplaced

some copy which had to be set in type that very day in order[1] to get into the evening paper. He was in a miserable state, and well he might be! Because he mislaid[2] the copy, an important ad was omitted from the evening papers, which meant that his employers would[3] have to stand a loss of thousands of dollars.

In all fairness, though, we cannot place all the blame on this printer. Some[4] of it must go to the fellows who write the copy. If they had sent the copy in a week before it was due[5] instead of mailing it on the final day, this mishap could have been prevented. If the printer is given a[6] little time, he can discover many errors and correct misprints so that when the job is finished it is correct[7] in every detail. Besides, he will be able to send you a proof so that you can make any changes[8] you like.

I know we can depend on you to get your December copy in without delay. Sincerely yours, (179 standard words)

Dear Sir: I cannot refrain from writing you what a fine impression your display made. I am glad you replaced the[1] old display, as most of the men with whom I had spoken disliked it I realize that it is unreasonable[2] to expect you to arrange a display that will please everyone, but your first display was far from perfect.

I[3] notice you discharged the young lady who had charge of the correspondence. She had not made such a good impression[4] on any of the men for whom she worked and I think you did the right thing. If you have not yet replaced the young lady[5] perhaps I may be able to help you get someone who will be an asset to you. I have three girls in my[6] office who are fine workers, but I find that I shall have to let one go. She is a hard worker and perhaps you[7] might care to talk to her. She would be a great help in your department. Cordially yours, (155 standard words)

Dear Sir: Owing to your unreasonable delay in reaching a decision, we had to refer several[1] complaints to the railroad company. If you had made your decision sooner, we could have taken care of these complaints[2] right here in the office. The railroad company states that it cannot grant a refund for the goods that were mislaid[3] on the train nor can it replace the goods that were stolen at the depot.

Much as I dislike the railroad[4] company's decision, I think its action is very fair. In most instances, the railroad company can be[5] depended upon to review any complaints and differences and settle them with dispatch. When the company[6] discovers an error, it is always willing to repair it.

If possible, I should like to keep these complaints[7] from the railroad company. We can do this if you will make your decisions promptly. All you need to do is sign[8] your name below mine on each letter as it comes to you. Yours very truly, (169 standard words)

ASSIGNMENT 33

161. I will be able, you will be able, he would be able, I should be able, to be able, has been able, I may be able, he received, I told you, upon the, several times, they received, I believe, I cannot believe, for the, if you would, there will be, I have not been, if you will, I have given, for them, to be, to plan, to blame, to feel, to find, to form, from the, about the, in which, and which, I would like, very much, to the, to them, he did not, I would not, you could, into this, into that, has been, as well as, as low as, as great as, to like, to which.

162. Was not, it was not, I was not, he was not, he wasn't, there was not, it is not, is not, he is not, which is not.

163. Record, advertise, previous, occasion, quantity, hundred, improve-improvement, acquaint-acquaintance, nevertheless-envelope, insure-insurance, educate-education, difficult-difficulty, newspaper-inspect, sufficient, merchandise, determine, pleasure, catalogue.

164. Reading and Writing Exercise

THE STORY OF PRINTING

Did you ever stop to think that there was a time when there were no printed books, newspapers, and catalogues? It is[1] difficult to realize that hundreds of years back there were no newspapers in which a man could advertise his[2] merchandise. There were no books from which he could get ideas and improve his knowledge of many subjects.

Business today[3] could hardly be carried on if the printing press had not been invented. Our whole educational system[4] is based upon the printed page and it is difficult to determine how schools would get along without a[5] sufficient quantity of books.

Think back for a minute over the ages previous to the invention of the[6] printing press. Writing in some form is almost as old as the human race, but the various means of recording[7] thoughts and ideas before the printing press were very crude. The first writing of which we have any knowledge is[8] picture writing. With picture writing, though, it was difficult to record quickly and completely the thoughts of the people.[9]

The next stage was the representation of sounds by different symbols. This was an improvement, but it was[10] not altogether satisfactory because of the difficulty of keeping records. During the Middle[11] Ages, a genius invented the quill pen. He acquainted the public with the fine qualities of the pen as[12] a writing tool and sold hundreds of them. He pointed out that it was a pleasure to write with the new pen and by[13] taking advantage of all the advertising media with which he was acquainted, he soon collected a[14] mint of money.

Whole books were copied with this quill pen during the Middle Ages. On many occasions an author[15] had to copy his entire book word by word with this quill pen and I think it is safe to say that it was not[16] a very enjoyable task. Nevertheless, some authors in the Middle Ages wrote as many as ten or[17] twelve books.

The coming of the printing press made many changes. Almost all books and newspapers which we have today[18] are printed from type of some kind. Yet the first printing from movable type took place hundreds of years back. The printing[19] in the early days was not always perfect, but it improved year by year.

A man in Europe is given credit[20] for inventing the art of printing. The first type he used was made of wood. He was not long in discovering that[21] wood was not satisfactory, but he was a man who knew no defeat. Next he tried carving type out of metal.[22] Even the printing from this metal type was not very clear, but it was still another improvement in the art[23] of printing. This man had the spirit of a winner and he had a definite influence on future progress[24] in this field. Another difficulty was conquered when a man printed a catalogue from type made of melted[25] lead. (501 standard words)

Dear Sir: Yesterday your new agent called to see me. As

I was not at home, he left an envelope with a[1] catalogue and some advertising matter. If you would be good enough to ask this new agent to call again, I[2] should like to get acquainted with him. It is always a pleasure to talk to a man representing your company.[3]

I already carry hundreds of dollars' worth of insurance, but one can never determine whether even[4] that much is sufficient. Up until a year ago, I was not insured at all. I soon realized, though, that I[5] was not doing the right thing. Very truly yours, (108 standard words)

Dear Sir: Thanks for your fine order of February 18. As this is the first occasion you have had to order[1] a quantity of our merchandise, we wish to point out to you how quickly the goods are shipped.

We receive hundreds[2] of orders like yours and each one is given immediate attention—each order is shipped the same day that[3] it is received It is not our plan to hold shipments and whenever the occasion arises we hire more men to[4] take care of the business.

I am going to be in your section of the city on April 16. I wonder[5] if you would be good enough to have luncheon with me on that day. I shall call you on the telephone and make[6] any arrangements that have to be made. Yours truly, (129 standard words)

CHAPTER VII

ASSIGNMENT 34

165. Debts, favorable, depart, matters, wanted, called, generally, descend, carried, charged, looking, explanation, reporter, thanks, requires, objection, satisfies, according, perfection, copying, approximate, dissatisfied, industrial, credited, removed, advantages, decided, remarks.

166. *(a)* Sudden, deny, dinner, evidence, hidden, condense, widen. *(b)* Tender, tendency, written, threaten, bulletin, straighten, captain, fountain, maintain, contain, obtain, retain, detain, attain, continue, continued, continues, continuous.

167. *(a)* Random, freedom, kingdom, seldom, academy. *(b)* Estimate, victim, emple, temporary, attempt, item.

168. To me, to my, to meet, to mean, to know, to make, it must be, it may be, at any, at any time, in due time, in due course, what to do, to draw.

169. Reading and Writing Exercise

A Friendly Visit

I had not seen Captain Temple for many years. I had written him many times, but he had never written to[1] me.

I seldom had occasion to look into the mail box because the maid I hired temporarily always[2] emptied the box, but today I happened to glance into the box, and there I saw what appeared to be a[3] bulletin hidden at the bottom of the box. It was not a bulletin—it was a letter to me from Captain[4] Temple! In it he asked me to spend several days with him.

As the Captain was a good friend of mine, I started[5] immediately to make arrangements to obtain my freedom from the office for a week. I estimated[6] that it took me three hours to straighten out my affairs, although I almost lost my temper when several people[7] attempted to detain me.

The distance to my friend's home was great, and I did not

know what to do with my time while[8] on the train. After dinner, I continued looking for news items that were of any importance. On the train[9] I met a little maiden in a blue cotton costume. I discovered that this little girl was bound for an[10] academy in a distant city. I pondered over the wisdom of sending this little girl all alone, without[11] any one to meet her at the end of her trip. At any time she might be the victim of some mishap.

The [12] train finally got to my town. All of a sudden a timid man stepped up to me and said the Captain had sent[13] him to meet me. This little man was a close friend of the Captain and was in continuous attendance at the[14] Captain's residence.

My heart missed a beat when I saw again the tender face of the Captain and I will not deny[15] that a tear rolled down my cheek. The Captain at once made me feel at home. He took me around his little kingdom[16] and showed me the tennis courts, the fountain in his back yard, and the mountains beyond. It must be heaven living near[17] these mountains all year round.

The Captain had made a trip to every continent of the globe and he loved to tell of[18] the dangers through which he had gone. The Captain's tales were hair-raising, even though he told them in condensed form.

My[19] temporary stay was soon over and I had to leave. My esteem for the Captain has increased greatly and I am[20] already making plans for another visit next autumn. It is a great pity that good friends should be obliged[21] to live so far apart. (424 standard words)

Dear Madam: Enclosed you will find our new bulletin, which came off the press yesterday. The bulletin contains an[1] itemized list of the autumn costumes that may be obtained here. Every sentence of the bulletin gives[2] evidence of our intense desire to be of help in any way we can.

Come in tonight or at any time and[3] inspect these costumes. Perhaps you may be able to make suggestions that will make these costumes more desirable.[4]

May we see you soon? Yours truly, (85 standard words)

Dear Sir: You may remember that about a year ago we sent you a bulletin telling you about our[1] durable bags selling for $19.50. The bags have been selling right along, but we now find it[2] necessary to clear out the entire stock of this model, and therefore we are selling the few remaining bags[3] for less than half the price mentioned above.

As we have only a few of these bags left and as this notice is going[4] to thousands of our friends, those who delay sending in their order may be too late. Act quickly!

The enclosed[5] bulletin will give you an idea of what this bag looks like. Yours truly, (113 standard words)

ASSIGNMENT 35

170. Ready, reader, readers, leader, leaders, many, manner, manners, any, near, nears, day, dare, dares, tea, tear, tears, me, mere, she, sheer.

171. I do not, I do not see, I do not know, I do not believe, we do not, we do not believe, they do not, they do not know, you do not, you do not know.

172. I don't, we don't, they don't, I don't believe, I don't know, we don't know.

173. Abstract, accommodation, accompany, administration, affidavit, afraid, American, application, approval, architect, argument, assist, Atlantic, attach, attorney, attract, authoritative, automobile, avoid, bankrupt, bookkeeper, bureau.

174. Reading and Writing Exercise

A Sacrifice

Bob and Nell were twins. I do not believe that one ever tried to do anything without the approval of the[1] other. They were very much attached and assisted each other whenever they could.

All through their school life they maintained[2] this tender regard for each other. I do not think I ever saw Bob that he was not accompanied by[3] his sister.

In due course these children finished high school. Nell went to an American academy to complete[4] her education. Bob was not sure whether he would become an architect or an attorney as he was[5] attracted by both professions. I am afraid that if Bob had not written a letter every day to his sister,[6] she would have been greatly annoyed. Bob wrote how the school administration had urged him to take up bookkeeping[7] and how he finally made an application for the course. I do not know whether this bookkeeping course appealed[8] to Bob very much, but he was not able to avoid it.

All went well for the first year. Suddenly, in the[9] autumn of the second year, both parents were killed in an automobile crash. This meant that one or the other must[10] discontinue school, as there was not enough money for both of them to go on. I do not believe I would know[11] what to do in this situation, but Nell decided at once that her brother's education came first, and after[12] considerable argument she persuaded him to continue his studies. Nell was glad to make this[13] accommodation even though anyone could see that she was sorry to have to leave school.

She kept Bob happy and[14] helped him with his studies. He talked over with her his most intimate plans and if she did not agree with him he[15] dropped them at once.

Had Nell given up too much when she left school after her parents had that automobile crash while[16] driving near the shores of the Atlantic? I do not think so. I spoke to many of her friends about this and they[17] did not think so.

Bob soon got to be a fine attorney and could speak authoritatively on matters having[18] to do with abstracts and affidavits. He had charge of a bureau that dealt with bankrupt organizations[19] and there was no one with a broader knowledge of law than he.

Bob always remembered what his sister had done for him[20] and he took care of her for many years, until he saw her happily married to an attorney friend of his.[21] (420 standard words)

Dear Madam: The abstract promised to me by my attorney accompanies this letter. I am sending it to[1] you for your approval. I realize that this abstract ought to have been mailed sooner but the delay could not be[2] avoided. You will notice that the abstract is in affidavit form.

I am afraid that the American[3] Bureau on Marketing will not give its approval to the contents of this abstract, and therefore the administration[4] of our organization has decided to send it to you and ask for suggestions. It may be that[5] by changing a clause or two the Bureau may accept it.

I do not know what we shall do if the Bureau finally[6] decides to withhold its approval.

I know we can count on help from every member of our organization,[7] all the way from the bookkeeper to the man in charge of the entire department. Very truly yours, (158 standard words)

Dear Sir: Thank you for writing me so promptly about your class at the college. I had hoped to visit you on Monday,[1] but I have been sent on the road, and therefore I will not be able to see you for more than a month.

Under[2] another cover I am mailing you several books that I should have liked to present to you personally,[3] but as I shall not see you this will not be possible. A copy of each of these books should be in the hands of[4] your boys and girls. I know they will enjoy the humorous way in which the subject is handled.

Very often a[5] dull subject can be made humorous by a proper treatment of the subject matter. You will notice how well written[6] these two books are, how they avoid monotony, and make the reader want to read more and more.

I should like you[7] to send me your reaction to these books. As I am not going to be in the office for a time, please write me[8] at my hotel. Sincerely yours, (165 standard words)

Assignment 36

175. Automobiles, avoid, attract, bureaus, attorneys, accommodations, assists, approval, application, Atlantic, American, unafraid, bookkeeper, records, improvements, undelivered, approximately, disappear, credited, indirectly, uncovered, industrial, disadvantage, required, answering, reports, valueless, carried, unemployed, asked, opinions.

176. Earn, burn, burner, cheer, cheered, shared, germ, shirt, charter, barn, bird, period.

177. Art, cart, guard, garden, smart, lard, alert, flirt, merit, guarantee.

178. Conceit, concert, deceit, desert, siege, serge, insert, insertion, assert, assertion, research, absurd, concern, third, thirty, thermometer.

179. (*a*) Large, larger, march, margin, argue. (*b*) Turn, term, serve, reserve, deserve, preserve, servant, verse, reverse, converse, learn, certain, firm, confirm. (*c*) Corner, born, court, cord, board, boarder, indorse, source, sort, warm, warn, worry, worth, worthy, worst.

180. Reading and Writing Exercise

Molly Pitcher

Molly Pitcher was a smart and alert little girl who served bravely in the war of 1776.[1] She was born on a large farm and spent part of her life on a farm. Every day she could be seen wheeling a little[2] cart in her flower garden or making nests for the birds that made their home in the barn.

When Molly was sixteen,[3] she took a position as servant to an army general. She learned quickly and it never took her a long[4] period of time to absorb anything that was told to her. Molly varnished the surfaces of tables and[5] repaired chairs. Her cooking was a source of delight to the reserve officers and she deserved their high praise.

Molly's[6] expert cooking and her charming manner brought many suitors for her hand and one day she married a young man by[7] the name of John Hays. Molly and John shared their joys and sorrows for quite a long period of time, but then the war[8] broke out and John wanted to serve his country. He and Molly would often converse about the war and he was surprised[9] to learn how much Molly knew about certain phases of army tactics. Suddenly an urgent call came for[10] John to leave. Molly cheered him and sent him off in search of his general.

A month passed until one morning she received[11] a message to return to her own people on the farm. She did this gladly, as John was a gunner in the[12] reserve of soldiers that was placed there. She saw her brave gunner many times and was allowed to search for him at the[13] scene of the battle.

One afternoon the thermometer reached 90. In this heat a great battle started and John[14] turned to the cannon he was to handle and got ready. Because of the heat, Molly marched to the battle front with[15] buckets of water for the soldiers. Each time she appeared the soldiers would cry for joy, "Here comes Molly and her pitcher."[16] Soon they changed that to "Here comes Molly Pitcher," and that name remained for thirty years after.

Suddenly the warm[17] sun caused John to faint—the burden was too much for him. Molly surveyed the situation, ordered two men to place[18] John under a large shady tree, and argued the general into letting her serve in John's place. At first the[19] general was firm, but Molly finally convinced him that she could handle the gun.

Bravely she picked up the rammer,[20] fired with all the nerve of an expert gunner. For hours Molly guarded the gun until the enemy was driven[21] back. The general warmly thanked Molly for her worthy deeds and from that day on she was known as "Captain Molly,"[22] the little maid who carried water to the fighting soldiers. (450 standard words)

Dear Sir: I was glad to get your inquiry of January 12 in which you express a desire to study[1] drawing. We are starting a new term next month, and therefore your inquiry came at the right time. An individual's[2] progress in our school is limited only by his own merit. You can finish the course in one year if you care[3] to work hard enough.

When you finish our course, we don't expect to be able to place you in a job that will pay[4] $75 a week. I would not be telling you the truth if I told you that you could go out tomorrow[5] and get a position as the head of some art division because you took our course. You couldn't do it. I[6] am telling you the truth, though, when I say that you will be equipped for a responsible position when you leave[7] us.

If you really like to draw, it is not fair to let your talent die out while others who have taken advantage[8] of their talents are holding fine positions that you might hold.

Mr. Brown, who has charge of the art work in this[9] school, has written a book on the achievements of our friends. Many are holding responsible positions that pay[10] a fine salary. I am sending you a copy of the book. Please read about these men and women who have been[11] successful in a field that seems to appeal to you. Cordially yours, (232 standard words)

ASSIGNMENT 37

181. Sudden, dinner, widen, written, bulletin, straighten, kingdom, freedom, estimate, temple, item, attempt, guard, guarantee, merit, period, large, indorse.

182. Western, eastern, attorney, eternal, fraternity, pattern, modern.

183. Neither, gather, mother, brother, weather, bother, leather, hitherto.

184. Christmas, citizen, civil, clerk, commerce, commercial, compare, comparative, consequent-consequence, conclude, conclusion, congress, connect, conspicuous, constitution, conversation.

185. Reading and Writing Exercise

Dear Robert: Yesterday I had a conversation with the clerk in the office and he tells me that we shall have[1] three days for our Christmas holidays. Because of this I cannot make that journey north with you. I am going to[2] visit my mother and father. One of my fraternity friends has a big modern car and has promised to drive[3] me home.

In May I came to the conclusion that I should like a civil service appointment, and consequently[4] I studied for the position of clerk of the court. Before an appointment is made a candidate must prove that[5] he is a citizen, but I had no difficulty in that regard.

I have been going to night school every[6] night and I am becoming quite an expert in commercial subjects. I am now studying the commerce of the[7] eastern and western parts of this country. Congress has recently passed several laws that will have an important[8] bearing on the commerce of these sections.

Somehow it is difficult to connect Christmas with the comparatively[9] warm weather we are having here. I had hoped that we would have a white Christmas, with snow covering the streets.

In[10] conclusion, let me wish you a very Merry Christmas.

Cordially yours, (212 standard words)

Dear Martin: We all missed you on Christmas. There was a terrible blizzard here the night before and we enjoyed the[1] white Christmas of which you wrote. The snow storm did not compare with the one we had once before, but there was plenty of[2] snow on the ground.

You were the chief subject of our conversation. We were all pleased to learn that you had been appointed[3] clerk of the court. You deserve every success and I know you will handle the position well.

My brother was[4] among those who gathered around the dinner table on Christmas and he said that the wages he was getting did[5] not compare favorably with those received by civil service employees. He was seriously thinking of[6] turning to civil service work.

Dick is getting to be an expert writer of verse. You may remember at one[7] time he was thinking of studying to become a teacher of history. He knew a good deal about the[8] Constitution and was well fitted for the job. He decided, though, that he would rather write poetry than teach. Dick[9] has been conspicuous at the meetings of the Writers' League and was picked to head the organization.

Write me[10] when you will have another vacation and I can guarantee you a warm welcome. The boys want me to wish you[11] a Happy New Year. Sincerely, (225 standard words)

Dear Mr. Wilson: We received an order from the Brown Company for several carloads of leather. We are[1] sending this order to you today, but please do not ship them any more leather until you hear from us. We have[2] not yet received a remittance from them for the goods shipped on October 30.

We learned today from a[3] reliable source that the firm is bordering on bankruptcy and that its eastern mills are not running.

I was surprised[4] to learn of this because all their machinery is modern and they did business with many large organizations[5] in this country. We have been selling them a large assortment of goods for a period of eight or nine[6] years and our dealings with them have been very satisfactory. Still, this doesn't warrant our selling them now if[7] payment cannot be guaranteed. We are very much concerned about this and will write you again. Yours truly, (159 standard words)

Gentlemen: I have made several comparative statements of the commercial affairs of our company. Before[1] I made these comparative statements I had a conversation with two members of Congress and several[2] attorneys.

I have come to the conclusion that I should file these comparative statements with the clerk and have them[3] considered immediately. I think this is possible under the Constitution of our country. Yours truly,[4] (81 standard words)

Dear Sir: I am glad to give you my opinion of James Barnes. The young man has been in our employ for eighteen months[1] as manager of the sporting goods branch of our store. He has attended faithfully to his duties and has shown[2] himself prompt and courteous. We are sorry to lose his services. Yours truly, (54 standard words)

ASSIGNMENT 38

186. Citizens, clerks, compares, commerce, approval, avoid, conclusions, Congress, Constitution, attorney, afraid, arguments, attract, consequences, connects, Christmas.

187. Forecast, forever, forget, forgive, forgot, forgotten, forenoon, forego, foreign, furnace, furnish, furniture.

188. Dignify, gratifying, notify, certified, fearful, grateful, helpful, beautiful, careful, cheerful, faithful, painful, powerful, successful, thankful, thoughtful, useful, wonderful.

189. Herself, himself, itself, myself, yourself, ourselves, themselves, yourselves.

190. Average, carriage, cottage, damage, discouraged, encouraged, encouragement, image, manage, manager, marriage, message, package, passage, patronage, percentage, storage, tonnage, village.

191. Reading and Writing Exercise

THE FURNACE

Since my marriage I have lived in a beautiful little cottage in the country. I could live in that cottage forever[1] if it weren't for one thing—taking care of the furnace. I could forget the hour it takes to get to the[2] office in the morning; I could overlook the task of mowing the lawn myself to make the land look dignified;[3] but I get terribly discouraged when at six each morning I have to attend to the painful and dreadful duty[4] of lighting the furnace.

At six in the morning it takes the greatest of will powers to get a strong grip on[5] ourselves, climb fearfully out from under the covers, and make the trip down to the furnace.

If you have a son your[6] task is sometimes simplified, but not always. The average boy does not have the courage to do this job himself[7] and it is not long before he gets discouraged. Even the most tempting bribes could not make him undertake the task[8] cheerfully a second time.

When evening comes, though, we forgive the furnace all the trouble it has caused in the[9] morning and relax in the gratifying warmth that it furnishes.

The man who furnishes us with a furnace[10] that can take care of itself will have a statue dedicated to his honor by the furnace tenders of this[11] country, and each year on his birthday they will betake themselves to his shrine and sing his praises.

The garage of our[12] cottage has no furnace and the family car usually feels almost as cold as I do when I take the daily[13] trip to the basement. Every morning when I step on the starter I am convinced that the car will spend its[14] next winter basking in the warmth of a storage house. As each year rolls around, though, I say to myself, "This winter[15] cannot be as bad as the last and I do not see how I can manage to get along without the car." True, each[16] winter wasn't as bad as the previous one—it was invariably worse.

Every day I may be seen[17] thoughtfully reading the real estate sections of the newspapers; I may be seen talking to managers of apartment[18] houses and looking over the furniture of the various rooms; I may be seen talking with dignified[19] agents about rents. Why these strange doings? I am going to give up my little cottage in the country village;[20] I am going to forsake the furnace and move to an apartment in the city where I can, by keeping the[21] janitor well supplied with cigars, get all the heat I care for.

I know when I'm licked   (436 standard words)

Dear Sir: After a careful inspection of our records, I find that you did not notify us when you sent us[1] your certified check. The check was mailed to the wrong department and therefore we had no way to trace it.

We are grateful[2] for the promptness with which you mailed this certified check, but I wonder if you would be kind enough to send all[3] future remittances to me. When I receive the remittance, I can take it personally to the man in[4] charge of your account and have him take care of it immediately.

If we can be helpful to you in any[5] way, send us a message outlining what we can do. You have been kind enough to give this company a fair[6] percentage of your business and we do value your patronage. Very truly yours, (134 standard words)

Dear Sir: On April 16 the manager was thoughtful enough to give you several days' leave so that you might[1] take care of your personal affairs. At that time it was my thought that you would be gone four or five days at the most[2] and that you would be back on the job again by the end of this week or the early part of next week.

I confess[3] I was a little puzzled when I received your airmail letter saying that you would have to remain away a[4] whole month. If this had happened at any other time, I should have had no objection, but as you know, this is the[5] busy season in our work and we need the help of every man on the force.

Would it not be possible for you[6] to return to the office immediately, and settle your personal business at some other time? I think[7] we can get the important business finished in about a month. After that, things will begin to slow up and you[8] can take as much time as you like.

I have spoken to the manager about your case and he feels as I do that[9] if we are to run this division successfully, all orders must be shipped the same day they are received. If you[10] are away, the orders are held up because the only man who can take over your work is Mr. Jones and he[11] has his hands full with his own work.

If, for some reason, you can't return, please wire me so that I may make plans for the[12] immediate future. Sincerely yours, (247 standard words)

Assignment 39

192. Standing, suggested, industrial, obligations, enabled, regularly, forced, except, unarranged, trustee, wires, inside, points, lightly, effects.

193. To him, I told him, we told him, give him, write him, tell him, I hope, we hope, I hope to hear, I hope you will, I hope you can, we hope you will, we hope you will be, we hope you will have, I am sorry, we are sorry, I want, you want, we want, if you want, do you want, early reply, at an early date, days ago, weeks ago, months ago, years ago, week or two ago, day or two ago, year or two, year or two ago, as soon as possible, few days, few months, few minutes, be sure, we are sure, I am sure, I feel sure, we feel sure, we were, you were, they were, we were not, you were not, they were not.

194. Corporation, coupon, crop, cultivate, curious, deceive, default, defendant, democrat, designate, disagreement, disappoint, discuss, distinct, distinguish, disturb.

195. Reading and Writing Exercise

The Uncovered Blackboard

Several days ago I was greatly amused when I read of the

discovery of a list of names that was[1] written fifty-two years
ago. This curious discovery made me think and disturbed
my sleep for a day or[2] two.

According to the story, the mayor of the town had a dis-
cussion with the school committee and decided[3] to designate
a corporation to tear down the old school and build a new
one. The workmen tearing down the[4] building uncovered
an old blackboard which, I am sure, had not been used for
many years. This board probably had remained[5] in a room
unnoticed or the teacher did not consider it necessary to re-
move it. At any[6] rate, there it was.

Now this may not seem so unusual to find an old board in
the back of a school room. But here[7] hangs the tale—at the
top of the board were, perfectly written, the years 1881-1882.
Under[8] these dates was a list of the names of the boys and
girls who had to remain after school that evening for[9] whispering. The writing was very plain and distinct, as it had not
been erased at the time the board was put away.[10] All through
the years these names had remained in place.

As I read the list of names, I wondered what had become of
all those[11] children who so many years ago had to stay after
school for having whispered to their neighbors. I wondered,
too,[12] if what they said to each other was important enough
to merit keeping them after school. I am sure they, at[13] least,
did not consider it so.

I noted that there was only one boy's name on that list.
This is another proof[14] that women of even tender years have
simply *had* to talk! You can be sure that Julia and Ann were
disappointed[15] because they had to remain after school. But
I wonder whether they refrained from whispering after their
names[16] were put on the board or whether a few days later

they were punished again. I wonder if the teacher remem-
bers[17] putting these names on the board and if she could distinguish one girl from the other.

Every day our names are[18] being written upon some board
and they will continue to stand there unless they are erased—
and we need not deceive[19] ourselves. What is written on the
board depends on the deeds we perform and if we want to
write a good record[20] on that board we must play the game
of life fairly and squarely.

But as the record of these children was finally[21] removed
with the tearing down of the building, so all records of wrong-
doing may be torn down. We want to forget[22] them as soon
as possible. (445 standard words)

Dear Sir: I hope it will be possible for us to settle the disagreement over the crops that were cultivated[1] by the farmers
of this section. We are sure you do not want to default on
the payment of the notes that[2] fall due in a few months. I
am sorry I cannot see you today as I am the defendant in
a case that[3] is being tried this afternoon. Do you want to
discuss this matter with me tomorrow? Perhaps we can
issue[4] coupons of some sort to the farmers whose crops are
concerned. Very truly yours, (93 standard words)

Dear Mr. Johnson: I am sorry I could not give your letter
an early reply, but I did not get to the[1] city until a few days
ago. I hope you will pardon the delay.

I wanted to discuss with our manager[2] the matter you
bring up, but he had to disappoint me because of another
engagement. He had to attend[3] a rally in his home town,
as he is a staunch Democrat.

I shall write him of the action I am suggesting.[4] I have
already given him a general idea of the situation, but I think

it is a good[5] plan to tell him about it again.

I was disturbed and disappointed when you designated a new man to[6] assist you in your work. I think this will be a distinct handicap to you, as it will now be necessary[7] to train this man from the beginning. Sincerely yours, (149 standard words)

Brief Forms

21.

28.

41.

49.

63.

72.

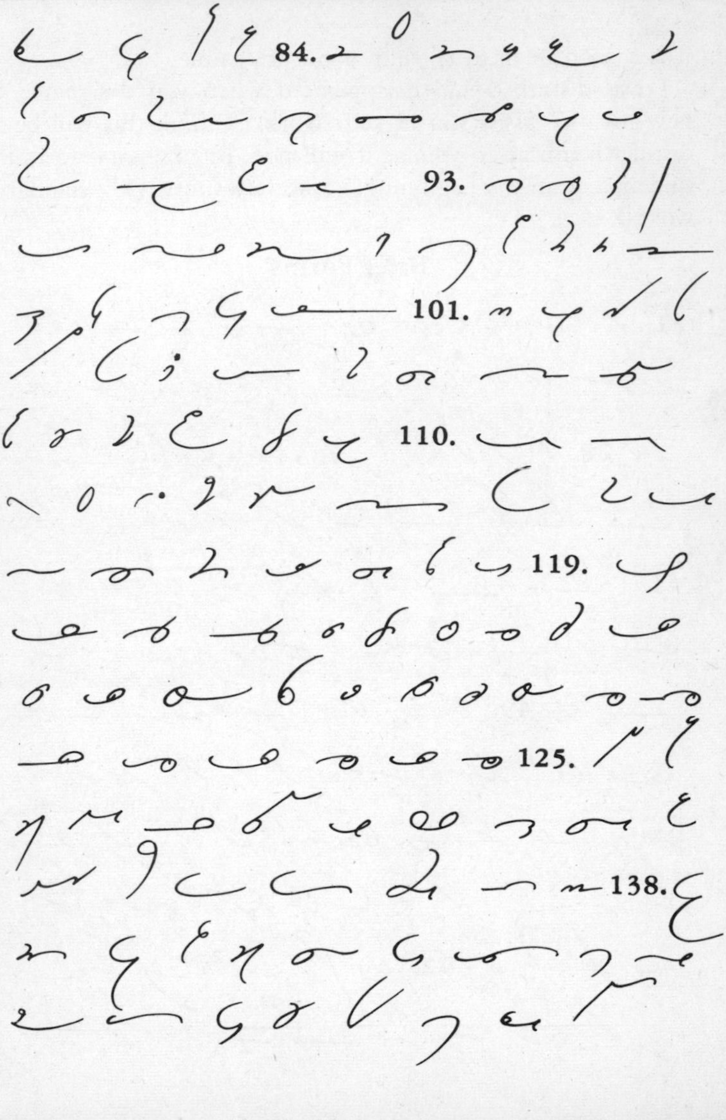
84.
93.
101.
110.
119.
125.
138.